STUDENT DRAMA SERIES

General Editor: MICHAEL MARLAND, B.A.

YOU AND ME

YOU
AND ME

FOUR PLAYS BY ALAN PLATER

SELECTED AND EDITED BY ALFRED BRADLEY

SENIOR DRAMA PRODUCER
B.B.C. NORTH

With a Note on the Media by ALAN PLATER

BLACKIE *LONDON & GLASGOW*

Blackie & Son Limited
BISHOPBRIGGS
GLASGOW G64 2NZ

5 FITZHARDINGE STREET
PORTMAN SQUARE
LONDON W1H 0DL

FIRST PUBLISHED 1973
ISBN 0 216 89577 4

PRINTED IN GREAT BRITAIN BY
WESTERN PRINTING SERVICES LTD., BRISTOL

 CONTENTS

A NOTE ON THE MEDIA

One of the big changes in the writing profession during the twentieth century has been the breakdown of the compartments in which individual writers work. In the grand old days, you were either a novelist, a poet or a dramatist and you stuck to your trade; writers who worked in more than one medium were unusual.

With the decline of the printed word and the development of the mass media—radio, television and films—writers are a much more versatile gang. Whether they are better writers is impossible to say and I don't propose to try. What is true beyond reasonable doubt is that the full-time professional writer needs to develop his ability in as many areas as possible. At the lowest level, he needs to do this simply to make a living; at the highest level, he needs to do it to become better at his trade. Writers like John Hopkins, David Mercer, and Harold Pinter would, I am sure, confirm that working in radio or television helps their work in the theatre and vice versa. It is simply a question of using as many creative muscles as possible. For the same reason, professional soccer players often play out of their real positions in training—Bobby Charlton is said to be a keen and gifted goal-keeper in these backstage situations—because it helps them to see their Saturday problems from a different angle. So it is with the writer.

Exactly how a writer applies this knowledge and experience in practice is harder to explain, because much of writing is an instinctive process. Bobby Charlton probably couldn't explain how he kicks a football—what messages his brain sends to his muscles and how the muscles respond to the instructions—all he knows is the ball is there and he kicks it. It is an instinctive reaction.

What I do know is that I spend as much time being a member of an audience as I do in writing plays. I listen to the radio, watch television and go to the theatre; and in writing for these media, my first thought is about the audience. Where are they sitting? What sort of room? Are they on their own? What are the distractions in the room? And, most important of all, what contribution will they make to the success of the play?

The audience for a radio play probably makes the biggest contribution of all. A radio play is composed of words, music, sounds, and no pictures. The audience has to make the pictures. The odd thing is that this does not present problems; the imagination of the radio audience is remarkable in its range and invention. Looking back on the finest radio productions of our time we find they are the programmes that leaned most heavily on this kind of contribution from their audiences—whether we think of Dylan Thomas's *Under Milk Wood* or the marvellous zany humour of *The Goon Show*. It is interesting that productions of *Under Milk Wood* on stage, and *The Goon Show* on television (with puppets), have been less successful than the originals.

Radio is not a prisoner of time or place. Scene One can be a street in Oldham; Scene Two a room in the Taj Mahal; Scene Three a space capsule on its way to Mars. You can go anywhere and do anything, in a way that is impossible on television and difficult in the theatre.

Radio is also a very personal and intimate medium. We are not eavesdropping so much on what people say as on what they think and *Excursion* is a good example of this. What we hear is not precisely what happens; it is one man's interpretation of what happens. It is not my world or your world but Norman's world; and a great many radio plays have this quality of being one man's (or one woman's) vision of a world that may be friendly, hostile or a mixture of the two. It is this personal quality—the ability to express an intimate and private vision—that has attracted so many poets to write for the medium: Dylan Thomas, Louis MacNeice, and Giles Cooper, who was very much a poet who carried a dramatist's union card.

Television is a much more earthy proposition. However much we preach about the rights and wrongs of the box, what it should or should not be doing, the plain fact remains: what television does best is to examine reality. Fairytales have little place on television and it is interesting that probably the best children's programme, *Blue Peter*, succeeds largely because it looks at the real world in a lively and interesting way.

The most effective television image is a close-up of a face—a refugee in India, a miner on strike in South Yorkshire, a politician under the studio lights, trying to shrug off an awkward question—faces that are smiling, shouting, angry, desperate, embarrassed or in repose.

It follows that television drama is built around the close-up, and generally around a small group of characters. We observe the changes in their relationship in close and precise detail; we see behind the eyes and read their thoughts. This technique can form the basis of plays containing extreme tension, like the John Hopkins quartet *Talking to a Stranger*, or of knockabout fun like *Dad's Army*. In each case the technique is the same: the close examination of human behaviour.

In a way *Seventeen Per Cent Said Push Off* lies somewhere between the two examples I have quoted. It is intended to be a comedy in the proper sense of the word; we should laugh at it, but only to stop ourselves crying. It was written to be produced in a television studio, so the settings are interiors that can be built in a studio, which in practice means the play has to happen within the confines of up to ten or at most a dozen rooms.

A similar discipline applied to *On Christmas Day in the Morning* which was written as a seasonal episode for the *Softly Softly* series. Here, however, there were also resources available for location filming—a normal technical trimming in what is to some extent an 'action' series.

There is an additional discipline involved in working for a series of course: the writer must share the assumptions of the series. If you are asked to contribute to a series about, say, district nurses, undertakers or chartered accountants, it would be foolish and dishonest to do so unless you have strong feelings about those professions. *Softly Softly* and its parent, *Z Cars*, have never been starry-eyed about the police force. The programmes have always said: policemen are people who are capable of courage, intelligence and sensitivity; but who are also capable of prejudice, misdirected violence and, in extreme cases, corruption. Because the series has always allowed its writers to examine the whole man, warts and all, it has maintained a high standard of writing, production and performance.

From that final comment, it is obvious that television depends on co-operation—between writer, actors, director and technicians. It is a team effort, and while this is also true of the other media, I think there is a difference of emphasis that might help to explain the writer's special problems. Radio depends on the listener, television on the creative team, and theatre? Very simple, this—theatre depends on the actor. However brilliant the text, the actor has the power to ruin everything on the night; conversely, many actors have given memorable performances working from scripts that should never have been allowed out of the dustbin.

Theatre involves the actor and the audience getting together and making magic; indeed, it is a kind of conspiracy. It is the only medium where a spectator can say to the actor: 'I think you're a terrible actor' (perhaps saying it silently)—and the actor has to do something about it.

This is best understood by thinking of a comedian like Ken Dodd or Frankie Howerd: every gag, every laugh-line, has to be timed and adjusted night by night according to how the audience reacts—and the comedian never knows in advance what the reaction will be. So it is for the actor, but in his case it isn't simply a matter of laughter, but of the rise and fall in tension, the building to a climax, the proper timing of a pause or a movement.

And a Little Love Besides was written for actors, first and last. The scenery is minimal. Again, we lean on the audience. The theatre must be transformed into church, assembly hall, living-room, courtroom, lakeside, without any physical help apart from lighting changes (which drop hints about atmosphere but little more). The job must be done by a conspiracy between actor and audience. It is rather like walking a tightrope—exciting, dangerous but in the end marvellously exhilarating.

This is not an easy or safe way to write plays, but it is built on the biggest single asset that the theatre can offer: the ability of the performer to say (like the stage illusionist) 'my next trick is impossible'—and then do it.

I should add, emphatically, that there are no rules about writing for radio, television or the theatre and most of the fun and excitement occur when writers break the rules; indeed, I would have written a different introduction five years ago, and will no doubt have changed my mind again five years hence. There are no certainties in writing as there are no certainties in life, and instinct is probably as reliable a guide as reason.

But this, roughly speaking, is what I think is going on when I tangle with radio, television and the theatre, and if it helps towards a clearer understanding of the plays, all the better. The humanity stays the same, whatever the wrapper; it's really about you and me.

ALAN PLATER

Excursion

A play for radio

CHARACTERS

NORMAN
TOM
ARTHUR
EDIE
DORIS
TERRY
PETE
SHEILA
BERNARD

✳ ✳ ✳
Excursion

A railway station platform. Trains, doors banging, football rattles, maybe a bugle. NORMAN is sitting in a carriage.

1 NORMAN. [*We are listening to his thoughts as we do throughout.*] An excursion train will depart from City Station at 10.35 arriving at 13.45 ... Returning at 23.43 and arriving back at City station at 02.56 ... proving ... it takes three minutes longer coming back than going ... how do they calculate these things? Why? Why do they bother? We're ... seven and a half minutes late already and we haven't set off. Special rate, thirty-five bob return, they just don't care, second class citizens ... refreshments will be available on the train ... we know what *that* means ... boozing and singing, vomiting even I shouldn't wonder. It gets the sport a bad reputation, and we've got declining attendances already ... [*He opens a newspaper.*] The stage is set for an epic gladiatorial contest as the gallant underdogs tackle the Midland giants ...

We leave NORMAN and cross fade quickly to a conversation in another part of the train.

2 TOM. As the gallant underdogs tackle the Midland giants ...

3 ARTHUR. Eh?

4 TOM. Tackle the Midland giants ...

5 ARTHUR. By God, they write some stuff, them fellers ...

6 TOM. It's a job, isn't it?

7 ARTHUR. When you read it out loud.

8 TOM. They're all alike. Rubbish. Our Edie likes it ...

9 ARTHUR. Doris's the same ...

10 TOM. They're all the same.

Cross fade to another part of the train.

1 EDIE. All murders, isn't it?

2 DORIS. Yes it is, isn't it?

3 EDIE. Shooting and strangling and goings on, they shouldn't put it in the paper . . .

4 DORIS. I like a good murder on the telly.

5 EDIE. Oh I don't mind that so much . . .

6 DORIS. I mean, it's the youngsters, really, hey look at that . . .

7 EDIE [*disapproving*]. I wonder who let them out?

Cross fade to another part of the train.

8 TERRY. Come on, beanbrain, over here . . .

9 PETE. Shuttup!

10 TERRY. Beanbrain.

11 PETE. I said beside the bookstall . . .

12 TERRY. Under the clock, you said. Who wants to buy books?

13 PETE. And you said . . .

14 TERRY. Lend us your comb.

15 PETE. Fancy yourself do you?

16 TERRY. Lend us your comb!

17 PETE. Here!

18 TERRY. I had to go back home for something, that's why I was a bit late . . .

19 PETE. What did you forget? Your head?

20 TERRY. Here . . . look . . .

21 PETE. Hey, you haven't brought . . . you mad-headed beggar . . .

22 TERRY. That's right . . .

23 PETE. You stupid . . .

A blast on the whistle and the train sets off.

24 NORMAN. Ten and a half minutes late, somebody should start a petition about it. It's a bit misty, is it? Is it mist? More what you'd call smokey, you get to expect it. Let's have

a look. They're very quiet. [*He looks at the newspaper.*] Dry with sunny periods, scattered showers later . . . dying out. Must be smoke then. Not mist. Good. Funny. They're very quiet opposite. Pretty girl. Watch yourself Norman!

Cross fade to another part of the train.

2 SHEILA. Bernard

3 BERNARD. Yes.

4 SHEILA. Is it like important?

5 BERNARD. What?

6 SHEILA. This football match.

7 BERNARD. Yes. Very important.

8 SHEILA. I thought it must be, the way you . . .

9 BERNARD. Went on about it?

10 SHEILA. I mean in a nice way.

11 BERNARD. It's a cup-tie.

12 SHEILA. Oh, is it?

13 BERNARD. Yes.

Pause.

14 SHEILA. What's that?

15 BERNARD. They're playing for the F.A. Cup.

16 SHEILA. You mean if Rovers, is it Rovers . . .?

17 BERNARD. Rovers, aye . . .

18 SHEILA. If Rovers win, they get a cup?

19 BERNARD. No.

Pause.

20 SHEILA. I just thought . . .

21 BERNARD. If they win, they play somebody else, and then somebody else and . . . like a knockout tournament . . .

22 SHEILA. Oh, like University Challenge?

23 BERNARD. Sort of.

1   SHEILA. I like that.

2   BERNARD. Then the two teams left, they play at Wembley, and
    the winners get the cup.

3   SHEILA. Wembley?

4   BERNARD. It's a big like stadium . . .

5   SHEILA. I know Wembley. It's when they sing Abide With Me.

6   BERNARD. That's right.

    Pause.

7   SHEILA. I've never seen a football match.

8   BERNARD. What about Wembley?

9   SHEILA. On the telly I saw that . . . just them singing the
    hymns, that's all.

10 BERNARD. Football's the best part really, I mean, that's what
    it's for . . .

11 SHEILA. It's a nice hymn, I like it, that and Eternal Father.

    Cross fade to another part of the train.

12 TOM. Remember Wolverhampton, don't you?

13 ARTHUR. Wolverhampton?

14 TOM. Don't you?

15 ARTHUR. I remember Wolverhampton all right.

16 TOM. Could happen again today.

17 ARTHUR. Funny game, football . . .

18 TOM. Especially the Cup.

19 ARTHUR. Aye, especially the Cup.

20 TOM. What it says here . . . hey, listen. Rovers' brilliant left
    winger, Dave Cummings . . .

21 ARTHUR. Let's have a look . . . brilliant?

22 TOM. Lads in the shop call him Nellie . . .

23 ARTHUR. Only uses his left leg to stand up on . . .

24 TOM. I'll tell you something. Dave Cummings, he'd never
    have got in the team that played at Wolverhampton . . .

1 ARTHUR. Might have let him pump the ball up, that's all . . .

2 TOM. Remember that goal Sid Curtis scored? Thirty yards out and . . .

3 ARTHUR. Who?

4 TOM. Sid Curtis, blond-headed kid, went to Queen's Park Rangers . . . the second goal, thirty yards out . . .

5 ARTHUR. Sid Curtis?

6 TOM. Went to Queen's Park Rangers.

7 ARTHUR. Alf Johnson, came from Derby County.

8 TOM. No, not Alf Johnson . . .

9 ARTHUR. Second goal at Wolverhampton. Rightfooted, first timer.

10 TOM. Sid Curtis couldn't kick with his right foot.

11 ARTHUR. That's why it was Alf Johnson. Liked his beer.

12 TOM. Well I'm not going to argue . . .

13 ARTHUR. No point in arguing . . .

14 TOM. It was a great goal . . .

15 ARTHUR. Great goal.

   Pause.

16 TOM. I'll not forget Wolverhampton in a hurry.

   Cross fade.

17 EDIE. They say it's a lovely shopping centre, our Joan says . . .

18 DORIS. I know, our Albert, the one that had shingles, he was saying, it's noted for woollens . . .

19 EDIE. Is it really?

20 DORIS. Woollens, yes . . .

21 EDIE. Well most places are noted for something . . .

22 DORIS. Here it's woollens . . .

23 EDIE. Fancy.

24 DORIS. So when Arthur said about the excursion, I said to myself, well . . .

1 EDIE. You did right Doris . . .

2 DORIS. Like he looked a bit sideways at me but . . .

3 EDIE. So did Tom. As long as you don't come to the match, he says, you can do what . . . [*quietly*] what the hell you like.

4 DORIS. Do you know, I've never heard your Tom swear.

5 EDIE. Haven't you?

6 DORIS. Never.

7 EDIE. Comes in fits and starts. Doesn't bother for ages and then it all comes in a rush, like a flood.

8 DORIS. I know, yes . . .

9 EDIE. Like this afternoon, it'll be like that. Referees, that's what sets him off mostly, referees.

10 DORIS. I don't think Arthur likes them very much either.

11 EDIE. Hey, do you need any?

12 DORIS. What?

13 EDIE. Do you need any woollens?

14 DORIS. I don't know. I won't really know till I see some.

    Cross fade.

15 SHEILA. How do you know which is Rovers?

16 BERNARD. You tell by the colours.

17 SHEILA. What sort of colours?

18 BERNARD. Like red and green and things like that.

19 SHEILA. I know but which ones?

20 BERNARD. Rovers wear red shirts and white shorts.

21 SHEILA. I see. [*Pause.*] All the time?

22 BERNARD. How do you mean, all the time?

23 SHEILA. Every time they have a match?

24 BERNARD. All teams do, they all wear the same colours for every match, more or less . . .

25 SHEILA. Bit funny, isn't it?

1   BERNARD. What's funny?

2   SHEILA. Bit boring, always wearing the same thing.

3   BERNARD. They're all fellers, fellers don't bother about things like that.

4   SHEILA. What about the other team?

5   BERNARD. United?

6   SHEILA. Is that who they're playing?

7   BERNARD. United, aye . . .

8   SHEILA. What colours?

9   BERNARD. Green.

   Pause.

10 SHEILA. Don't much like red and green together. They should never be seen . . . my mam says . . .

   Cross fade.

11 TERRY. Dave Cummings . . .

12 PETE. What about him?

13 TERRY. He's a big nancy.

14 PETE. Is he heck as like.

15 TERRY. He's a bigger one than you and that's saying something.

16 PETE. Shuttup.

17 TERRY. So's mine, must be the weather. Cummings.

18 PETE. Best winger they've got.

19 TERRY. Our mam could play a better game than him.

20 PETE. Scored last week.

21 TERRY. Aye, with his backside.

22 PETE. He never did.

23 TERRY. He flaming did, you know.

24 PETE. Give over.

25 TERRY. Said in the paper, a skilful deflection by Cummings. You what? Nudged the ball with his bum as it went past.

1 PETE. You're talking rubbish.

2 TERRY. He nearly died of fright when it went in. He blushed.

3 PETE. Rubbish.

4 TERRY. I'm telling you, he blushed. True as I'm riding this bike. Blushed. I've never seen nowt like it.

5 PETE. Different match to the one I saw.

6 TERRY. You know your trouble.

7 PETE. What?

8 TERRY. You don't know nothing about football, no eye for the subtleties.

9 PETE. Give over.

10 TERRY. Only to be expected, you being so thick to begin with . . .

Cross fade.
The train noise fades up under NORMAN's *thoughts to punctuate the scenes in the train.*

11 NORMAN [*reading*]. Rovers' main hope rests with unorthodox left winger, Dave Cummings, approaching the veteran stage but still liable to surprise defenders with . . . [*Pause.*] Veteran? He's only . . . thirty-two. What's that make me, if you're a veteran at thirty-two? Never did like this paper. Pretty full, the train, should be a good gate. They've brought their wives with them. No place for a woman, a cup-tie. I wouldn't take my wife to a cup-tie. That's . . . if I had a wife. Dave Cummings approaching the veteran stage and he's thirty-two and I'm forty-five and haven't got a wife. But it's no place for a wife, a cup-tie. [*Pause.*] Anyhow, he was a bloody awful left winger when he was twenty-seven.

Cross fade.

12 EDIE. As a rule I don't bother.

13 DORIS. Neither do I.

14 EDIE. Because it's not all it makes out . . .

1 DORIS. Well I remember them pillowslips, did I tell you about the pillowslips . . .?

2 EDIE. And anyhow I looked and it said special offer and I thought well, that seems . . .

3 DORIS. How much did you say?

4 EDIE. Eighty-nine pence.

5 DORIS. Is that all?

6 EDIE. And I thought, well, that seems . . .

7 DORIS. With the extra one?

8 EDIE. Three altogether.

9 DORIS. Well, you're bound to, aren't you?

10 EDIE. Special offer, what I mean is, it *was* special . . .

11 DORIS. At eighty-nine pence . . .

Cross fade.

12 TERRY. Six for tenpence.

13 PETE. Is that all?

14 TERRY. Special offer.

15 PETE. Didn't know you went shopping . . .

16 TERRY. Getting some bread just, for the old lady, backhander in it, like. Anyhow, there they were, six for tenpence, row upon row, so I got a packet. Stuck one on the lav, two in the kitchen cupboard, three in my pockets . . .

17 PETE. Start chucking toilet rolls they'll have you out of the ground.

18 TERRY. You what? Beanbrain.

19 PETE. No messing, the scuffers'll have you.

20 TERRY. Thirty thousand people watching, who'll know who pelted it? Hands up who slung the toilet roll? Give over . . .

21 PETE. Balmpot.

22 TERRY. Anyhow, it's only if Rovers score, and everybody's going to be watching the goal when that happens.

1 PETE. It won't happen.

2 TERRY. I got three of these things, kid.

3 PETE. You won't need them.

4 TERRY. I'm telling you. Three one.

5 PETE. Rubbish.

6 TERRY. I'm not going all this way to watch them get a good hiding.

7 PETE. Well, it's hard luck 'cause that's what they're going to get.

  Pause.

8 TERRY. Let's see your money.

9 PETE. Money?

10 TERRY. You say a good hiding, I say three one to Rovers, let's see your money.

11 PETE. All right then. [*Pause.*] How much?

12 TERRY. A note.

13 PETE. A quid?

14 TERRY. I'm not bothered, my money's safe.

  Pause.

15 PETE. Right then.

16 TERRY. Right then. [*Pause.*] Pity about that twirp Cummings being on the left wing.

  Cross fade.

17 BERNARD. What you thinking about?

18 SHEILA. You like football, don't you?

19 BERNARD. Yes.

20 SHEILA. Funny, isn't it?

21 BERNARD. No.

22 SHEILA. Oh. [*Pause.*] I like Gene Pitney.

23 BERNARD. Do you?

1   SHEILA. Well, you know where you are, don't you? With Gene Pitney, anybody like that, or else The Stones.

2   BERNARD. What's it got to do with football?

3   SHEILA. Same as the pictures, you know what's on before you go, you know what it's going to be like . . . football you can't tell.

4   BERNARD. That's the fun, that's what makes it so exciting.

5   SHEILA. What?

6   BERNARD. The uncertainty.

7   SHEILA. They might lose.

8   BERNARD. I know. They'll probably lose today.

9   SHEILA. If you think that, why did you bother coming?

10   BERNARD. They might not.

11   SHEILA. That's why . . . ?

12   BERNARD. If they win it'll be terrific, I want to see it . . . Rovers only Third Division, and them First Division, you see?

13   SHEILA. I suppose it's daft really, it's nothing like Gene Pitney at all . . . what's Third Division mean?

     Cross fade.

14   TOM. When he saved the penalty?

15   ARTHUR. At Wolverhampton, aye . . .

16   TOM. I remember, shot straight at him, didn't he? O'Leary it was, Irish international, shot straight at him . . .

17   ARTHUR. No, he had to move to his left . . .

18   TOM. Hardly.

19   ARTHUR. At Wolverhampton you're talking about?

20   TOM. That's right, just before half-time it was . . .

21   ARTHUR. Just before half-time, that's right . . .

22   TOM. Well it was straight at him.

23   ARTHUR. Moved to his left . . .

24   TOM. I don't want to argue but . . .

25   ARTHUR. I'm not sure he didn't dive.

1   TOM. He definitely didn't dive.

    Cross fade.

2   NORMAN [*reading*]. Rovers are a well known cup-fighting side, best remembered for their two nil win over Wolverhampton Wanderers in the fourth round of the cup twenty years ago . . . [*Pause.*] Twenty years ago? Can't be twenty, now there was the Festival of Britain and then . . . yes, twenty years. [*Pause.*] Another ten minutes, we'll be there. Twenty years, it's a long time from one bit of glory to the next.

    Cross fade.

3   ARTHUR. And then they got knocked out next round, played like girls.

4   TOM. At home, an' all.

5   ARTHUR. Right let-down was that.

6   TOM. Swindon Town.

7   ARTHUR. Eh?

8   TOM. Swindon Town.

    Pause.

9   ARTHUR. Darlington.

10   TOM. Darlington.

11   ARTHUR. Darlington.

    Pause.

12   TOM. Are you sure?

13   ARTHUR. Darlington, at home. Three nil.

14   TOM. Funny. [*Pause.*] I just have a kind of sensation, you know, it might have been Crewe Alexandra.

    Cross fade.

15   EDIE. We'll have to arrange a place to meet.

16   DORIS. After the match.

17   EDIE. Yes, after the match.

1 DORIS. Else we'll lose them.

2 EDIE. Once we lose them, we'll never find them.

3 DORIS. Arthur!

4 EDIE. They're talking.

5 DORIS. They never stop.

   Cross fade.

6 NORMAN. Three miles to the station it said near that signal-box . . . Five minutes. If we were going sixty miles an hour it'd be three minutes. A mile a minute. But we're not. Not even thirty miles an hour now . . . very slowly, you could say, signals it'll be. I'll put my coat on all the same.

   Cross fade.

7 SHEILA. We'll have to stand up?

8 BERNARD. I thought you knew . . .

9 SHEILA. I thought there'd be sitting down . . .

10 BERNARD. There is but you've got to get tickets and . . . costs a bit . . .

11 SHEILA. How long for?

12 BERNARD. Couple of hours.

13 SHEILA. Just in case they win.

   Cross fade.

14 TERRY. Hey, beanbrain!

15 PETE. What?

16 TERRY. You carry that one.

17 PETE. Get knotted.

18 TERRY. Go on, can't have them all under my coat, I look seven months gone . . .

   Cross fade.

19 NORMAN. You can never tell . . . it could be like Wolverhampton again.

Cross fade.

1 TOM. Just hope for the best.

2 ARTHUR. All you can do.

    Cross fade.

3 SHEILA. I hope it doesn't rain.

4 BERNARD. Doesn't rain at football matches.

5 SHEILA. But if it does . . .

6 BERNARD. Get wet.

    Cross fade.

7 TERRY. Hurry up, get to the door . . .

8 PETE. Last on, first off . . .

9 TERRY. Naturally . . .

10 PETE. What's the hurry?

11 TERRY. If we're going to tear this place apart . . .

12 PETE. Madhead.

13 TERRY. Beanbrain.

    Cross fade.

14 EDIE. Have you got your purse love?

15 DORIS. Yes. I brought a rain hat, did you?

16 EDIE. I've got a scarf I can use.

    Cross fade.

17 NORMAN. And please Lord, make Dave Cummings have one of his good days.

    The train draws to a halt at the station.
    Fade out.

An explosion of pre-match shouting, rattles, bugles, maybe a band playing. Fade down, almost to silence, under NORMAN's *voice.*

18 NORMAN. Good crowd, lot of Rovers people here. Good view,

I did right to come straight here from the station. If it wasn't for this chap in front I'd have another sandwich only . . . he wouldn't want tomato down his neck. And I think he's one of theirs . . .

Crowd, as before, fading up.

2 TOM. All right, are you?

3 ARTHUR. Aye, I'm all right, are you all right?

4 TOM. Aye, I'm all right.

5 ARTHUR. That's all right then.

6 TOM. Must be forty thousand here, more than Wolverhampton.

7 ARTHUR. Never in the world.

We leave ARTHUR *and* TOM *and cross fade to another part of the ground.*

8 BERNARD. You'll be all right once they get started.

9 SHEILA. I'll believe you, thousands wouldn't.

10 BERNARD. It's funny, once it starts . . .

11 SHEILA. I must be a bit simple . . .

12 BERNARD. What for?

13 SHEILA. Like if I can't see now, how's it all going to change, will they all go home or something?

Cross fade.

14 TERRY. I can see smashing, can you?

15 PETE. All right, I'll manage.

16 TERRY. Good lobbing distance.

17 PETE. There's a lot of coppers round the pitch.

18 TERRY. What of it?

19 PETE. They'll be watching, that's what of it . . .

20 TERRY. Unruly elements in the crowd, that's all they're bothered about.

21 PETE. Like you.

1   TERRY. I'm not unruly, just enthusiastic.

    Fade out.

Fade in to atmosphere of a large departmental store. Chatter and an occasional cash register.

2   EDIE. Thank you very much.

3   DORIS. Ask her about the woollens.

4   EDIE. Where's your wool department please?

    Fade out.

An explosive cheer as the team comes out.

5   NORMAN. Here they come.

6   TERRY. Come on Rovers, you great daft twits!

7   TOM [*quietly*]. Right lads, let's be having you.

8   PETE. Come on Rovers, you useless shower!

9   ARTHUR. Take it steady, nice and steady.

10   SHEILA. I can't see.

11   BERNARD. Rovers have come out.

    Fade crowd noise.

12   NORMAN. Trotting out, muscular, confident, on to the field. Limbering up, sprinting, kicking, heading, rolling their sleeves up. They always look good before the match, Rovers, it's the best part of their Saturday. Look at Dave Cummings, shooting in. Traps the ball like Matthews, smooth and easy, two strides, then thrashes it into the net like Bobby Charlton, younger of the famous footballing brothers from Ashington, Northumberland. Always looks good, Cummings, when he's practising. Hasn't scored in a match proper for two and a half months.

    Fade up crowd noise.

1 TOM. We've won the toss.

2 ARTHUR. Happen it's the only thing we will win.

3 TOM. I don't know so much. Remember what happened at . . .

4 ARTHUR. I know, I know . . .

   Cross fade.

5 SHEILA. Did you say that's us in red?

6 BERNARD. In red, yes.

7 SHEILA. They're prettier than the others.

8 BERNARD. They're a very pretty team.

   Cross fade.

9 TERRY. Come on then Rovers, stand on them.

10 PETE. Get stuck in.

11 TERRY. Anything above grass.

12 PETE. They can't run without legs.

13 TERRY. No messing, get stuck in.

   A blast on the whistle then fade crowd.

14 NORMAN. And straight from the kick-off, Rovers are defending. Not muscular any more, not confident any more. Tough, dogged, chasing everything, but the green shirts keep swarming back . . . and Rovers goalkeeper has to dive at the centre forward's feet and gets winded . . . and their inside right hits a first time shot and it hits the crossbar, and nobody sees it at all . . . and their right winger gets the ball and looks dangerous so two Rovers players trip him up at the same time because they can't stop him any other way . . .

   Fade up crowd.

15 TERRY. He's given a free kick, he never touched him.

16 PETE. One-eyed flaming referees . . .

17 TERRY. Always favouring the home team. Get stuck in Rovers.

1   PETE. He tripped himself up, ref.

2   TERRY. Having a lot off to the ref, he is. Shuttup, you lippy
    devil!

3   PETE. Paid fifty thousand pounds for him, they did. Get
    stuck in.

4   TERRY. Wouldn't give fifty thousand washers for him, right
    pansy.

    Cross fade.

5   SHEILA. He's got nice fair hair.

6   BERNARD. You what?

7   SHEILA. He's got nice hair.

8   BERNARD. Can't possibly have, he's on their side.

    Cross fade.

9   TOM. Struggling a bit, Arthur.

10 ARTHUR. Aye, just a bit.

11 TOM. Takes time to get adjusted to the pace.

12 ARTHUR. That'll be it.

13 TOM. Hey, look at that.

14 ARTHUR. Bit hasty, that.

    Cross fade.

15 TERRY. Send him off.

16 PETE. Send him off.

17 TERRY. Dirty swine.

18 PETE. Right mucky do, isn't it?

19 TERRY. Fouling hound.

20 PETE. What did he do?

21 TERRY. I didn't see.

    Cross fade.

22 TOM. Real cup-tie stuff.

23 ARTHUR. Rough as hell.

1   TOM. First-time tackling, straight in, bang.

2   ARTHUR. Hard luck if you get in the way.

3   TOM. It's grand to watch.

    Fade crowd.

4   NORMAN. Twenty-five minutes gone and Rovers beginning to attack. Not really dangerous, more what you'd call hopeful. Optimistic. Hit hard and hope. Up and under. Kick and rush. Speculative belts. Thump it down the middle and run like hell. Then, suddenly, with a rush of blood to the head, somebody rolls the ball neatly, quietly along the ground to Dave Cummings on the wing.

    Fade up crowd.

5   TOM. Fancy giving it to him.

6   ARTHUR. Get a move on with it . . .

7   TOM. Standing there gawping . . .

8   ARTHUR. Fannying about.

    Cross fade.

9   TERRY. Look at him the great girl.

10   PETE. He's beaten the full back.

11   TERRY. He's just stood there.

12   PETE. Get rid of it.

13   TERRY. Boot it.

    Cross fade.

14   TOM. Push it down the wing.

15   ARTHUR. Centre forward's waiting for the pass.

16   TOM. He's going to shoot.

    Cross fade.

17   TERRY. Shooting from right out there . . .

18   PETE. The nit, the steaming Scottish nit!

Crowd noise cut, to silence.

1 NORMAN [*quietly*]. And Cummings shoots, from thirty yards, and he scores.

Fade out.

Fade in to the departmental store.

2 EDIE. Which do you like best?

3 DORIS. I like the beige, I think.

4 EDIE. That fawn's nice.

5 DORIS. They're both nice really.

6 EDIE. I like the beige as well.

7 DORIS. That's a pretty one, what is it?

8 EDIE. Terracotta it says on it.

Fade out.

Fade in to the crowd cheering.

9 TOM. What a lovely goal.

10 ARTHUR. Goalie never saw it.

11 TOM. Like a flaming rocket.

12 ARTHUR. With his wrong foot.

Cross fade.

13 BERNARD. Did you see it? Did you see it?

14 SHEILA. That was a goal wasn't it?

15 BERNARD. I'll say it was.

16 SHEILA. I thought so . . .

17 BERNARD. A beauty.

18 SHEILA. Was that our side? Was it the red ones?

Cross fade.

19 TERRY. Cummings, you're the greatest.

1   PETE. He's the greatest all right.

2   TERRY. Here we go.

3   PETE. Hey stoppit!

4   TERRY. We've scored a bloody goal, man, what do you expect me to do . . . come on the lads . . . !

Fade out crowd.

5   NORMAN. And a bit of trouble behind one of the goals, kids throwing toilet rolls. It's a pity, it spoils the game, gets a bad reputation for your supporters . . . policemen moving in, oh dear, oh dear, what a pity, what a pity. A lovely goal though. What a beauty! Dave Cummings, you'd have thought he was practising.

A blast on the whistle.

Half-time.

Fade out.

Fade in to café atmosphere, cups rattling, etc.

6   EDIE. Will you have another buttered scone?

7   DORIS. I shouldn't really.

8   EDIE. Go on, be a pig.

9   DORIS. All right then.

10   EDIE. Nice cup of tea.

11   DORIS. Very nice.

Pause.

12   EDIE. It's a nice colour.

13   DORIS. I'm glad you bought that, I liked it best.

14   EDIE. I'm glad you like it.

15   DORIS. What colour did she say it was?

16   EDIE. Cinnamon.

17   DORIS. Cinnamon.

1 EDIE. Dirty brown I'd call it.

   Fade out.

Fade in to street noises. We can hear the cheering from the match in the background.

2 TERRY. Beanbrain.

3 PETE. You're the beanbrain.

4 TERRY. If you'd kept your big trap shut.

5 PETE. He saw you throwing them.

6 TERRY. Did he heck as like! He was watching the match.

7 PETE. Rubbish.

8 TERRY. It was you saying 'It wasn't us, it wasn't us.' He's bound to be suspicious, isn't he? You saying that, you daft beggar.

9 PETE. I didn't pelt the flaming thing.

10 TERRY. That's got nowt to do with it.

11 PETE. Course it has.

12 TERRY. Flaming hasn't.

13 PETE. We're watching the second half out here in the street, right?

14 TERRY. What of it?

15 PETE. If you hadn't slung the toilet roll, we'd still be inside.

16 TERRY. It's not a bad street.

   A blast on the whistle.

   There they go. We can hear the cheers.

17 PETE. I could bloody well weep, do you know that? Weep.

   Pause.

18 TERRY. Go on then.

   Fade out.

Fade in to the crowd cheering.

1 TOM. I fancy 'em you know Arthur.

2 ARTHUR. Confident they are, now.

3 TOM. I know it's early days . . .

4 ARTHUR. It's early days but it could be . . . another Wolverhampton.

5 TOM. Another Wolverhampton.

6 ARTHUR. By heck. We've waited years.

7 TOM. Years and years.

   Cross fade. Fade crowd.

8 NORMAN. History might repeat itself. Rovers holding out with
   something to spare, only occasionally resorting to shirt-
   pulling, ankle-tapping and elbow-digging. Even then,
   they're more sinned against than sinning. It's United
   that's getting desperate now.

   Fade up crowd.

9 SHEILA. Why did the police do that before?

10 BERNARD. What?

11 SHEILA. With those lads . . .

12 BERNARD. Because they threw a toilet roll.

13 SHEILA. Why did they throw it?

14 BERNARD. 'Cause Rovers scored, they were happy about it.

15 SHEILA. Are you not allowed to be happy?

16 BERNARD. Only according to the rules.

17 SHEILA. Is it all right shouting what that feller was shouting?

18 BERNARD. What was he shouting?

19 SHEILA. I'll whisper.

   Fade out.

Fade in to the crowd cheering behind the noise of traffic.

1   TERRY. It sounds like a smashing game.

2   PETE [*sulking*]. Shuttup.

3   TERRY. So's mine, must be the weather.

    The cheers swell.

    Hear that?

4   PETE. What of it?

5   TERRY. Indirect free kick just outside the penalty area.

6   PETE. Who to?

7   TERRY. To Rovers.

8   PETE. Rubbish.

    More cheers.

9   TERRY. Don't make any odds, they made a muck of it.

10   PETE. Twenty minutes to go.

11   TERRY. It'll be all right, kid, don't worry. Listen. Offside . . .
    to them.

    Fade out.

Fade in to cheering, inside the ground.

12   TOM. Well I'm backing 'em.

13   ARTHUR. So am I.

14   TOM. Look at that. Lovely play, Dave.

15   ARTHUR. Playing well, is Cummings.

16   TOM. He's a good lad, good ball player, that's the thing.

17   ARTHUR. Usually are, from Scotland.

    The cheers fade.

18   NORMAN. Dave Cummings, the hero of Rovers. One week in
    ten they love him more than the Queen or Fountains
    Abbey. The rest of the time he's a cross between Charlie
    Drake and Mussolini. He's playing a lovely game. They
    all are, all playing a lovely game, better even than they

did that day at Wolverhampton. [*Pause.*] Until . . . until suddenly the centre half slips, and the centre forward gets the ball and he's clean through, churning through the middle towards the goal, and only Rovers' goal-keeper to beat . . . just the two of them and everything seems to stop.

Fade out.

Fade in to the sounds of a busy street.

2   EDIE. Where did we say we'd meet them?

3   DORIS. Town Hall steps.

4   EDIE. Town Hall, is it?

5   DORIS. Looks like a Town Hall.

6   EDIE. All big and black.

7   DORIS. It'll be the Town Hall.

8   EDIE. Along this way I think . . .

9   DORIS. We must have walked miles.

Fade out.

Fade in to an explosion of cheering behind the noise of traffic.

10   TERRY. It's a goal.

11   PETE. One all.

12   TERRY. Rovers have scored again, two nil . . .

13   PETE. One all.

14   TERRY. Two nil, you got no faith.

15   PETE. One all . . .

Fade out.

Fade in to the ground.

16   TOM. One all.

1 ARTHUR. Would you credit it.

2 TOM. They don't deserve it.

3 ARTHUR. They're a very lucky team.

4 TOM. One all. One flaming all.

Cross fade.

5 SHEILA. Bernard . . .

6 BERNARD. What?

7 SHEILA. What's the matter?

8 BERNARD. What's the matter? What's the matter? Don't you know?

9 SHEILA. I can tell there's something wrong.

Fade crowd noise.

10 NORMAN. United equalize. Three minutes to go and they equalize. Five thousand men, women and children want to cry. It's in the nature of a betrayal . . . like biting into a soft centre only to find caramel.

The final whistle.

It's all over. Daylight robbery. Daylight flaming robbery.

Cross fade.

11 TOM. Hell's teeth.

12 ARTHUR. It's a good job I left the dog at home.

13 TOM. Ours an' all.

14 ARTHUR. I'd boot it over yon stand.

15 TOM. Only three minutes to go . . .

Cross fade.

16 BERNARD. There was only three minutes to go.

17 SHEILA. I don't care.

18 BERNARD. Else we'd have won.

19 SHEILA. That's no excuse for language like that . . .

20 BERNARD. Yes it is . . .

1 SHEILA. If that's what football matches do . . .

2 BERNARD. Well they do! That's what football matches do!

Fade out.

Fade in street noises.

3 TERRY. One all.

4 PETE. I told you.

5 TERRY. I asked that feller. One all.

6 PETE. I told you. When we heard the cheers.

7 TERRY. Hard luck though, wasn't it?

8 PETE. We didn't see half of it, we don't know.

9 TERRY. Must have been hard luck. If it'd been ten one it'd still be hard luck.

10 PETE. You're a nut-case.

11 TERRY. Never mind. Half an hour and the pubs are open.

Fade.

12 NORMAN. And now we've all got to find something to do until 23.43 . . . twenty to midnight . . . wine, women and song. Ha ha. Have to find a café, all my sandwiches have gone soggy.

Fade in to street noises.

13 EDIE. You'll be able to tell by the faces.

14 DORIS. They're taking their time.

15 EDIE. You should see him come in when they've lost, slams the door, chucks his cap in the corner, dog goes under a chair . . .

16 DORIS. Course, there'll be a lot of people . . .

17 EDIE. I'll know, just have to look at the faces . . .

18 DORIS. Maybe had trouble getting on a bus . . .

1   EDIE. Is that them?

2   DORIS. Where?

3   EDIE. Across the road . . .

4   DORIS. Got the wrong glasses on, I'm still wearing my tea-
     drinking ones . . .

5   EDIE. That's them. Tom looks happy enough. Arthur looks
     as if he's had a nasty accident.

6   DORIS. Must have been a draw then.

     Fade out.

Fade in to the noise of a public bar.

7   TERRY. There's your wrestling.

8   PETE. You can stuff wrestling.

9   TERRY. There's a flower show . . .

10 PETE. You what?

11 TERRY. Oh no, that's tomorrow, cactuses it is, prize cactuses,
     it's a funny paper this . . .

12 PETE. Any dances?

13 TERRY. What do you think I'm looking for?

14 PETE. Give us the paper here . . .

15 TERRY. Get your filthy hands off . . . here we are . . . old
     time?

16 PETE. Don't be stupid.

17 TERRY. Very sexy, you can get raped in the Gay Gordons, it's
     a well-known fact. Here we are, the Majestic. Sounds
     like the place . . .

18 PETE. Eight o'clock.

19 TERRY. That's in about . . . six pints from now . . .

20 PETE. I've still got that other toilet roll.

21 TERRY. Hang on to it.

22 PETE. What for?

1   TERRY. You might want to wipe your nose.

Fade out.

Fade in to the sounds of a restaurant.

2   NORMAN. If I'd realized it was one of these . . . never mind . . . sweet and sour king prawns with boiled rice or chips . . . what's this one? Green Dragon Special with bamboo shoots, bean sprouts, egg, noodles, don't fancy that. Here we are . . . haddock, peas and chips. I wonder what they're having?

Cross fade to a nearby table.

3   EDIE. They all look nice.

4   DORIS. Our Natalie was telling me, she'd had something nice in one of these places, now what was it?

5   TOM. Curried hedgeclippings.

6   ARTHUR. There's some right stuff down here by heck.

7   EDIE. You'll like it.

8   TOM. Aye.

9   ARTHUR. Aye.

10 DORIS. What you having then?

11 EDIE. I don't know. What you having?

12 DORIS. What you having Arthur?

13 ARTHUR. What you having Tom?

14 TOM. I'll have what Edie has.

15 EDIE. I'm not all that hungry, we had them scones.

16 TOM. All right then, I'll have a Green Dragon Special.

Pause.

17 EDIE. You're not are you?

18 TOM. I thought I was for a minute.

19 EDIE. Do you think you'll like it?

1 TOM. Aye . . . as long as there's not too many dragons in it.

    Fade out.

Fade in to busy street sounds.

2 BERNARD. It's all right, the queue's moving.

3 SHEILA. About time.

4 BERNARD. It'll be warmer inside.

5 SHEILA. There's a lot of people coming out.

6 BERNARD. There's no queue at that one down the street.

7 SHEILA. Don't want to go there, it's an Italian film.

8 BERNARD. What about it?

9 SHEILA. Well it'll be in Italian, won't it?

10 BERNARD. I should think so.

11 SHEILA. They always are, I saw one on the telly.

12 BERNARD. Do you like Charlton Heston?

13 SHEILA. He's all right.

14 BERNARD. You know where you are with him, any road.

15 SHEILA. Oh yes.

16 BERNARD. Not like football.

17 SHEILA. Nothing to do with football.

    Fade out.

Fade in to the restaurant.

18 TOM. It was a lovely goal.

19 ARTHUR. A smasher it was, like a rocket.

20 EDIE. Good.

    Pause.

21 DORIS. Edie got some wool.

22 ARTHUR. Wool?

1   EDIE. I got some wool.

2   TOM. Good. She got some wool Arthur.

3   ARTHUR. Oh aye. Good.

4   TOM. Like . . . any special sort of wool?

5   EDIE. For knitting with.

6   ARTHUR. That's the best sort.

7   TOM. Always said so.

8   EDIE. Ask me what colour.

9   TOM. Oh aye . . . any special colour?

10   EDIE. Cinnamon.

> *Pause.*

11   TOM. Cinnamon?

12   EDIE. Yes.

13   DORIS. Show them it.

14   EDIE. It was very reasonable, apparently it's noted for wool . . .

15   ARTHUR. Sheep country.

16   EDIE. There we are.

17   TOM. Cinnamon?

18   EDIE. That's its name.

19   TOM. More like a dirty brown to me.

20   ARTHUR. Aye, just like . . .

21   DORIS. You're awful, you two.

> *Pause.*

22   TOM, Yes, very nice.

23   ARTHUR. When I was a lad, I remember we used to smoke cinnamon.

24   TOM. That's right, I remember.

25   ARTHUR. I don't remember knitting any.

26   EDIE. He was on the train, him that just went out.

> *Fade out.*

Fade in to NORMAN's *footsteps.*

1 NORMAN. Is it coming on to rain? No. Just thought, for a minute. Four hours yet. Should have stayed in that place longer but . . . didn't really want any coffee and those people at the next table . . . I think they were going to talk and . . . what if they had? . . . suppose it doesn't matter really. I wouldn't take my wife to a football match. But I haven't got . . . [*Pause.*] Pictures? What's this one . . . Italian . . . let's see the pictures . . . Oh dear it's one of those ones . . . so what's it matter, you're a long way from home . . . walking up and asking for the tickets, that's the hard part . . . there's one further along . . . [*He walks on.*] Bible epic. Bit of a queue though. Best . . . walk about a bit . . . think about it . . . plenty of time.

Fade out.

Fade in to the public bar.

2 TERRY. Who's buying?

3 PETE. You are.

4 TERRY. You are.

5 PETE. I bought the last.

6 TERRY. I bought some pies since then.

7 PETE. Pies don't count.

8 TERRY. They're not free you know, hot pies, shilling each.

9 PETE. It's your round.

10 TERRY. Rotten devil.

11 PETE. I'll have another pint.

12 TERRY. All right then.

Pause.

13 PETE. You're not moving.

14 TERRY. Haven't got any money, you'll have to lend me some.

1 PETE. You haven't got any money?

2 TERRY. Give us a quid, that'll do . . .

3 PETE. What if I say no?

4 TERRY. You'll have to buy me one.

Fade out.

Fade in to the cinema, we can hear the sound track in the background.

5 BERNARD. Are you all right?

6 SHEILA. Yes thanks. [*Pause.*] It's warm. I can see everything. I've got an ice-cream.

7 BERNARD. Same here.

8 SHEILA. Guess what it's better than.

Fade out.

Fade in to NORMAN's *footsteps.*

9 NORMAN. Summarizing then, we would seem to have, on the one hand . . . Charlton Heston in The Second Book of Kings . . . on the other hand, or, if you prefer it, at the dark end of the street . . . Sweet Passion in the Rice-fields with subtitles . . . it isn't easy, it isn't easy at all . . .

Fade out.

Fade in to the restaurant.

10 EDIE. How much longer are you going to be?

11 TOM. Plenty time.

12 DORIS. Just cause they found out it had a licence . . .

13 TOM. Well Edie doesn't like pubs.

14 ARTHUR. It's a fair drop of brown, this, to say it's bottled stuff.

15 TOM, Aye, it's not bad.

16 EDIE. There's some shop windows we haven't looked in yet.

17 ARTHUR. Shops aren't open.

1 DORIS. So you're quite safe, aren't you?

2 EDIE. There's the bill.

3 TOM. By heck Arthur, look at this . . .

4 ARTHUR. Let's see . . .

5 TOM. Three pound fifty . . .

6 ARTHUR. There's a place near the works, you can get hot pie, peas and chips for twenty, and that includes your bread and butter and tea . . .

7 EDIE. We're having a day out, it doesn't matter.

8 DORIS. If Rovers had won, it wouldn't have mattered.

9 ARTHUR. I've been thinking about that, Tom.

10 TOM. The match?

11 ARTHUR. I'm not so sure that goal they got wasn't offside.

12 TOM. I thought so at the time.

13 EDIE. Forget about football for five minutes . . .

14 TOM. Oh. We'll split this, Arthur . . . nice . . . nice bit of wool that was you bought, love.

Fade out.

Fade in to the atmosphere of a dance hall.

15 TERRY. It's a right place this, isn't it?

16 PETE. Like a battlefield, isn't it?

17 TERRY. Well, it's Saturday night, they're all looking for it.

18 PETE. What?

19 TERRY. If you don't know it's no good me telling you. That's all right, isn't it?

20 PETE. Not bad.

21 TERRY. Choosey. [*Pause.*] Well. No time to waste.

22 PETE. Off are you?

23 TERRY. Redhead. If we're leaving at eleven I'll have to be quick out of the traps.

1 PETE. All the best.

2 TERRY. I'll be all right, don't worry, kid.

Fade out.

Fade in to NORMAN's *footsteps.*

3 NORMAN. Sweet Passion in the Ricefields . . . seats in all parts . . . it's a woman in the paybox I don't think I could look her in the eyes . . . she'd know, she'd realize . . . Hey, there's a second feature . . . Naked and Unashamed now showing. [*Pause.*] Second Book of Kings. [NORMAN *hurries away.*]

Fade.

Fade in to four pairs of footsteps. EDIE, DORIS, TOM *and* ARTHUR *are window gazing.*

4 EDIE. They're nice . . .

5 DORIS. The bathtowels . . .

6 EDIE. Yes.

7 DORIS. Very reasonable as well.

8 TOM. It's noted for bathtowels, this place.

9 DORIS. Is it?

10 EDIE. Don't take any notice.

11 ARTHUR. It's noted for long streets full of shops.

Fade out.

Fade in to the cinema.

12 SHEILA. All right love?

13 BERNARD. Yes.

14 SHEILA. Enjoying it?

15 BERNARD. Yes.

16 SHEILA. Good. I'm glad you're enjoying it, I like biblical films.

1 BERNARD. Yes. [*Pause.*] Sheila . . .

2 SHEILA. Yes.

3 BERNARD. Sorry but . . . I've got cramp in my arm.

4 SHEILA. Oh have you . . . there . . .

5 BERNARD [*groans*]. Shoots right through you, right past my shoulder.

6 VOICE. Shhh!

Fade out.

Fade in to street sounds.

7 NORMAN. Funny. Nobody about. Nobody to sell me a ticket. You'd think they'd be only too glad to sell you tickets, it is their business, after all . . . wrong sort of attitude, ruins the export drive that kind of thinking. Let's see. [*Pause.*] I suppose he's right. People don't want to come in two thirds of the way through the film, last performance . . . [*sighs*] Half past nine. Two hours. If I walk very slowly to the station, then have a cup of tea there, buy a paper. Then the train might be there and I could sit on it. In it. That's the best plan. A slow walk.

Fade on NORMAN's slow walk

Fade in to the dance hall.

8 TERRY. Now then kid.

9 PETE. Hallo Terry, I thought you'd got fixed up.

10 TERRY. I thought so an' all . . .

11 PETE. Saw you dancing, doing things with your hands like and . . .

12 TERRY. She's got a feller here.

13 PETE. A feller?

14 TERRY. Engaged, he reckons.

15 PETE. What did she say?

1 TERRY. He seemed to think it was nothing to do with her.

2 PETE. Didn't you sort him out?

3 TERRY. He was about seven foot six.

4 PETE. Aim low.

5 TERRY. And he'd got about nine mates, and they were all seven foot six an' all . . .

6 PETE. I'm surprised at you Terry.

7 TERRY. Are you?

8 PETE. I am.

9 TERRY. Trouble is. It's playing away. Dead dodgey when you're playing away, this kind of thing . . . come here . . .

10 PETE. Where you going?

11 TERRY. Up on the balcony.

Cross fade into different dance music as they arrive on balcony.

That's it.

12 PETE. What you going to do? Hey, where'd you get that from?

13 TERRY. Your coat in the cloakroom.

14 PETE. You can't throw that in here . . .

15 TERRY. Bet?

16 PETE. We'll get slung out . . .

17 TERRY. Where is he?

18 PETE. Terry, you're a raving lunatic . . .

19 TERRY. That's right. There he is, by Hell, he's a good target, being so tall. . .

20 PETE. I'm off.

21 TERRY. Here we go. [*He slings the toilet roll.*] Good kid Terry, a direct hit. Poleaxed the bastard.

Fade out.

Fade in to NORMAN *walking.*

22 NORMAN. Longer walk than I thought. Good job I allowed

plenty of time. Only got ... an hour and forty minutes. Well, if I have a cup of tea ...

Fade out.

Fade in to the street.

2   TOM. Station's this way.

3   EDIE. Are you sure?

4   DORIS. There's the Town Hall.

5   ARTHUR. General Post Office.

6   TOM. General Post Office?

7   EDIE. We've been calling it the Town Hall.

8   TOM. Have you?

9   ARTHUR. General Post Office.

10   TOM. Ministry of Labour and National Insurance. And the station's up that way.

Fade out.

Fade in to BERNARD *and* SHEILA *walking.*

11   BERNARD. He played a storming game though.

12   SHEILA. What?

13   BERNARD. Dave Cummings.

14   SHEILA. Don't tell me, I know. He scored the goal.

15   BERNARD. Very good.

16   SHEILA. I think Charlton Heston's very good.

17   BERNARD. Yes, he is. Very good. [*Pause.*] Did you want to get a bus to the station?

18   SHEILA. I think I'd rather walk.

19   BERNARD. I'd rather walk as well.

20   SHEILA. Best thing if we walk then.

Fade out.

Fade in to PETE *and* TERRY *walking.*

1 PETE. Which way's the station?

2 TERRY. God knows, could be straight up for all I know.

3 PETE. You're a birk.

4 TERRY. Never dull though, is it kid?

5 PETE. Getting us slung out of the dance and the football match, it's not bad.

6 TERRY. Didn't half fetch him a crack, it did, the twit.

7 PETE. Wonder he didn't fetch you one.

8 TERRY. But he didn't know who it was did he?

9 PETE. Lucky for you.

10 TERRY. Wasn't watching was he?

11 PETE. That bouncer was watching though, wasn't he?

12 TERRY. He was a big kid wasn't he? Legs like tree trunks.

13 PETE. Where's the flaming station?

14 TERRY. I haven't got it.

15 PETE. If we miss the train . . .

16 TERRY. If we miss it, at least we won't get slung off it.

Fade out.

Fade in to the inside of the train.

17 NORMAN. Departing at 23.43 and arriving at City Station at 02.56 . . . still a bit worried by the three minutes difference between coming and going . . .

Cross fade.

18 EDIE. I'm tired.

19 DORIS. Been a long day.

20 EDIE. Not finished yet.

21 DORIS. Our Tony was going to leave our electric blanket on.

22 EDIE. I'll have my bottle, I like my bottle . . .

Cross fade.

1 TOM. Could have been, you know.

2 ARTHUR. Could very easily have been.

3 TOM. Just for that three minutes from the end . . .

4 ARTHUR. An offside goal.

5 TOM. And it would have been another Wolverhampton.

Cross fade.

6 SHEILA. You said it was one goal each.

7 BERNARD. Yes.

8 SHEILA. And you get a goal for kicking it between them posts.

9 BERNARD. Yes.

10 SHEILA. I saw them kick it between the posts three times.

11 BERNARD. They got one, it was disallowed. Somebody fouled.

12 SHEILA. Is that like cheating?

13 BERNARD. Like cheating.

14 SHEILA. And that feller standing behind me called the referee that . . . that word . . .

15 BERNARD. He did, didn't he?

16 SHEILA. What's it mean? That word? Exactly what does it mean?

A blast on a whistle.

17 NORMAN. 23.43 and away . . . and two lads sprinting down the platform, it shouldn't be allowed.

A door slams and the train sets off.

18 TERRY [*breathless*]. Bloodyell . . .

19 PETE. It's great going away with you.

20 TERRY. That's why I'm so popular.

21 PETE. Slung out of everywhere.

22 TERRY. We're on the train.

23 PETE. This is the way to the station . . .

1 TERRY. On the train, on our way home . . .

2 PETE. Going the wrong way, have to get a taxi.

3 TERRY. We're on our way home.

4 PETE. Have you got any money Pete? For the fare?

5 TERRY. What's up?

6 PETE. You're not fit to be out on your own!

7 TERRY. That's why I brought you with me.

Cross fade.

8 TOM. Coming back from Wolverhampton . . .

9 ARTHUR. Played cards all the way . . .

10 TOM. Sailors, weren't they?

11 ARTHUR. Sailors.

12 TOM. Solo.

13 ARTHUR. Brag.

14 TOM. I'm going to say it was solo.

15 ARTHUR. I've a recollection it was brag.

Cross fade.

16 EDIE. They're funny, aren't they?

17 DORIS. Them?

18 EDIE. Them.

19 DORIS. They're funny all right.

20 EDIE. I mean. They just live from one football match to the next. Keeps them going, somehow.

Cross fade.

21 SHEILA. Bernard love . . .

22 BERNARD. Yes?

23 SHEILA. I think another time . . . you go on your own to football matches . . .

24 BERNARD. Haven't you enjoyed yourself?

25 SHEILA. I've enjoyed it only . . . I think I'm wasted on a football match.

1   BERNARD. We'll go some other place next time.

2   SHEILA. I'd like that. [*Pause.*] I'll have to tell George.

3   BERNARD. George?

4   SHEILA. Just this lad, don't worry about it . . . I'll sort it out.

5   BERNARD. What lad?

6   SHEILA. Shhhh!

Cross fade.

7   NORMAN. The Saturday Green 'Un . . . Gallant Rovers surprise over-confident United. Late equalizer prevents
sensational victory . . . It seems about a million years ago.

Cross fade.

8   TOM. Funny, the women, they just live from one special offer
to the next . . .

9   ARTHUR. Aye, I've noticed. It's only shop windows keeps
them going.

Cross fade.

10 EDIE. Doris . . . did you see them lengths of curtain
material . . . ?

But all we hear is DORIS's *heavy breathing.*

She's asleep.

Cross fade.

11 BERNARD. Sheila . . . who is he?

But all we hear is SHEILA's *heavy breathing.*

Asleep.

Cross fade.

12 TERRY. Hey Pete . . . ?

13 PETE [*sleepily*]. Shuttup.

14 TERRY. Party on tomorrow night, are you coming?

15 PETE. Shut up.

44

1 TERRY. I'll come round in the morning, fix it up.

2 PETE. Shut up.

3 TERRY. Right then. I'll go see what's doing in the buffet car. Coming?

4 PETE. Shut up. No I am not. And you haven't got any money.

5 TERRY. Aye. [*Pause.*] Goodnight then.

   Cross fade.

6 TOM. Lovely goal.

7 ARTHUR. Cummings?

8 TOM. Aye.

9 ARTHUR. Nice pass from McDonald.

10 TOM. Murphy.

11 ARTHUR. I don't want to argue but I think you'll find it was McDonald.

12 TOM. Murphy. I've a feeling it was Murphy.

   Pause.

13 ARTHUR. Hang on. I think you're right, I think it was Murphy.

14 TOM. Eh?

15 ARTHUR. My mistake.

   Pause.

16 TOM. Are you sure it was Murphy?

   Cross fade.

17 NORMAN. Tomorrow, it'll be over, barring the Sunday papers. Over now really, till the replay next Wednesday. From one to the next to the next. It's a good trip, a football trip, when you win. When you lose, it's a hell of a long way back. When you draw . . . it's sort of ordinary, sort of grey. Not black and not white. Rovers, they have more black than white, on the whole. Mostly it's grey, just dull grey and ordinary. [*Pause.*] But we keep on watching, keep on waiting . . . waiting for the white. If you don't keep on going, you might miss it. [*Pause.*]

45

And there's nothing worse than knowing it's been . . .
and knowing you've missed it.

The train speeds into the night.
Fade out.

On Christmas Day in the Morning

A script from the B.B.C. television series 'Softly Softly'

CHARACTERS

DETECTIVE CHIEF SUPERINTENDENT BARLOW
DETECTIVE SUPERINTENDENT JONES
DETECTIVE CHIEF INSPECTOR WATT
DETECTIVE SERGEANT HAWKINS
DETECTIVE CONSTABLE MORGAN
DETECTIVE SERGEANT CONWAY
DETECTIVE CONSTABLE RANKIN
CHARLES WILSON
MURIEL WILSON
BRENDA REED (RECEPTIONIST)
YVONNE BALL
PAYNE
MRS PAYNE
JEFFREYS
HOTEL GUESTS, STAFF, ETC.

※ ※ ※

On Christmas Day in the Morning

THE SQUAD OFFICE   Day

Christmas Eve. The office has token rather than lavish decorations. MORGAN *has just come through from Barlow's office and is talking to* HAWKINS.

1   MORGAN. So then we had welcome to the Squad, D.C. Morgan, hope you have a long and successful career with us, God bless all who sail in you, type of thing . . .

2   HAWKINS. Mr Barlow made the speech?

3   MORGAN. That's right.

4   HAWKINS. Sounds like the usual rubbish.

5   MORGAN. All you *can* say . . . it's bound to be rubbish really . . .

6   HAWKINS. I'd say . . . sorry you got yourself in the Squad, you might not like it at first, but in time you'll learn to hate it . . . after about three days.

7   MORGAN [*deadpan*]. He didn't say anything about hating it. [*Pause.*] Will I?

8   HAWKINS. What?

9   MORGAN. Hate it?

10   HAWKINS. Three days.

11   MORGAN. At least I'll have a merry Christmas first . . .

12   HAWKINS. Did Mr Barlow say Merry Christmas?

13   MORGAN. Never mentioned it.

14   HAWKINS. Not even . . . come and have a drink with us later on?

15   MORGAN. Not even that.

16   HAWKINS. You'll like it here.

There should be an element of send-up in HAWKINS*'s sourness and* MORGAN *is aware of it.*

49

THE HOTEL CAR PARK Day
'Pentland Grange' Hotel —a large high-class hotel in a semi-rural setting. As the car park is filling up with holiday arrivals a large Rover 3.5 drives in. It moves smoothly to the main entrance where a COMMISSIONAIRE *opens the car door almost as soon as it stops.* CHARLES WILSON *and* MURIEL WILSON *get out of the car—just long enough for us to recognize them later on.*

THE CO-ORDINATOR'S OFFICE Day

BARLOW, JONES *and* WATT. *The atmosphere is very casual and relaxed—they could well be having a festive drink.*

1 BARLOW. Yes, I think we chose a good lad in Morgan.

2 JONES. He's got the right kind of ancestry.

3 BARLOW [*to* WATT]. He means Welsh.

4 WATT. I see. Is that good?

5 JONES. Now John, I don't want to start hitting people, not on Christmas Eve . . . which reminds me . . .

6 BARLOW [*saying it for him*]. Are we taking our boys out for a quick one . . . ?

7 JONES. I trust the answer's yes . . .

BARLOW *is already halfway to the door.*

8 WATT. I always thought the Welsh celebrated Christmas in August.

9 JONES. There's such a thing as the Race Relations Board, boyo.

THE HOTEL FOYER Day

WILSON *is signing the register. He is a man in his late thirties, expensively dressed, elegant and witty. There should be no hint of crookedness: he is much too professional for that. The* RECEPTIONIST, BRENDA REED, *smiles her welcome.*

10 BRENDA. Thank you, Mr Wilson, I hope you have a very pleasant holiday.

11 WILSON. I'm sure we will.

The RECEPTIONIST *calls to a* HALL PORTER *nearby.*

1 BRENDA. Room 128, please.

The PORTER *joins* WILSON *and* MURIEL, *who we assume is* WILSON'S *wife—slim, attractive and in her early thirties, and all three move towards the lift.*

THE SQUAD OFFICE Day

HAWKINS *and* MORGAN *are startled as* BARLOW *walks briskly and breezily into the office.*

2 BARLOW. Right lads . . . who's coming for a drink with the top brass? [*Pause.*] No volunteers? Oh, all right. . .

3 MORGAN. I'm prepared to volunteer, sir.

4 BARLOW. Hawkins?

5 HAWKINS. Thank you, sir . . .

6 BARLOW. Don't let's hang about.

BARLOW goes out. We hold the reactions of HAWKINS and MORGAN briefly, and then they follow him.

THE HOTEL FOYER Night

This time we see rather more than just the reception desk. We see that the hotel is decorated—if anything overdecorated—for the festive season. The foyer is the same room as the residents' lounge, which in its turn is linked to a cocktail bar—perhaps with implied divisions created by changes in level. WILSON *and* MURIEL *are sitting in the lounge casually taking in the scene, with special attention to the new guests as they enter and register.*

7 WILSON. It's a pleasant room they've given us.

8 MURIEL. Very.

9 WILSON. Delightful view.

10 MURIEL. It's a very pretty car park.

This is a private joke.

11 WILSON. Always best to choose one's room well in advance.

MURIEL picks up the hotel brochure.

1 MURIEL. Tonight we're having a grand Christmas Eve dance.

She makes it sound rather like a funeral.

2 WILSON. I love grand dances.

3 MURIEL. So we can all break the ice, get to know each other . . .

4 WILSON. Make exciting new friends . . .

5 MURIEL. Yes.

MURIEL looks across to a group of new arrivals; two men and two women, the LORD LIEUTENANT and a PARLIAMENTARY PRIVATE SECRETARY and their WIVES. They drip money, notably the fur coats worn by the women. Out of the distant hubbub of conversation, we pick up the RECEPTIONIST's voice.

6 BRENDA Room 236 and 242 . . .

PORTERS come rushing as we cut to reaction shots from the WILSONS.

7 MURIEL. They seem very exciting.

8 WILSON. Don't they just . . .?

And still their attitude is no different from that of anybody staying in a hotel and making snide remarks about strangers.

A PUB Night

The Squad local, early on Christmas Eve. Things are already quite boozy—though not the police contingent: BARLOW, JONES, WATT, HAWKINS and MORGAN, who are all very chatty and relaxed, but also very sober.

9 JONES [*scornful*]. Christmas? Just an orgy of self-indulgence . . .

10 WATT. That's why I like it.

11 BARLOW. And then of course we have the administrative problems . . .

12 JONES. Keeping the system going.

13 BARLOW. Exactly.

1 WATT. I feel sorry for the people that have to work through you know . . . vicars, undertakers, the weathermen . . .

2 JONES. Police?

3 WATT. Yes, I feel very sorry for them.

4 HAWKINS. I feel sorry for them all the time.

5 BARLOW. The Squad's a very tricky problem . . . you have to ask a man to give up . . . everything . . . in the cause of law and order. Difficult isn't it, Morgan?

6 MORGAN [*sensing conspiracy*]. Yes, sir, very difficult.

7 WATT. Very hard for those who have to make the decisions . . . who stays at home . . . who doesn't . . .

Pause. MORGAN *gives way under the pressure.*

8 MORGAN. Well I suppose, being the new boy . . . I . . .

An eruption of laughter from the others, including HAWKINS, *who isn't in the secret but has worked it out for himself.*

9 BARLOW. No, Morgan, you're very lucky. We've got somebody in the Squad without any responsibilities whatsoever.

They look at WATT.

10 WATT. All my life I've been lucky.

THE HOTEL CORRIDOR   Night

A corridor serving one of the upstairs bedroom wings. We see YVONNE BALL, *a chambermaid in her early twenties, who walks briskly along the corridor then stops beside a wall-mounted fire extinguisher. We are close enough to see exactly what she does. She fastens a key, a pass key, to the back of the fire extinguisher with a small piece of sellotape, then walks briskly on. No tension, no fuss. Just doing a job.*

THE PUB   Night

WATT *gets up to go.*

11 BARLOW. You're not going yet.

12 WATT. I've got work to do.

1 JONES. Spoiling the party.

2 WATT. I'm a great spoiler of parties.

3 JONES. What's all this about work to do?

4 WATT. I am giving up everything in the cause of law and order, remember ... [*Pause.*] Besides it's my round next. Compliments of the season everybody, and goodnight.

> WATT *goes. The party is a little subdued now, some of them wanting to leave but waiting for a lead.*

5 JONES. Well, who's having another?

6 MORGAN. I'd like to be getting home, sir, really.

7 JONES. Harry?

8 HAWKINS [*looking at his watch*]. Well ...

9 BARLOW. Wife and responsibilities ... yes, I know ... have to be off to my hot chestnuts and brown ale ...

10 JONES. Like I said, self-indulgence ... you miserable lot ...

11 BARLOW. Like John says, he's a great spoiler of parties.

12 JONES. Come on then, let's bow to the inevitable ... All the best, boys.

13 HAWKINS. And the same to you, sir ...

14 BARLOW. Yes. God bless us, every one ...

15 MORGAN. Thank you sir, all the best ...

> *The conversation is very jagged and informal and not helped by the crowded and boozy atmosphere in the pub where singing has now set in.*

16 BARLOW. And I don't want to see any of you before Friday.

THE HOTEL CORRIDOR   Night

WILSON, in evening dress now, walks up to the fire extinguisher, and takes the key. He walks on, again very quiet and undramatic.

THE HOTEL BALLROOM   Night

The Grand Dance has started. Tables are set, cabaret fashion, round a modest sized dance floor. The music is supplied by a small group. We explore the scene ending on MURIEL WILSON's *table. She sits alone as a* WAITER *crosses to her.*

1 MURIEL. I'll just have a bitter lemon, please.

The WAITER, *with impeccable politeness, implies a slight query in his look.*

I'd like to keep a clear head for a little while, anyway ... oh, and a whiskey and dry ginger for my husband ... one clear head should see us through the evening ...

THE SQUAD OFFICE Night

WATT *sits at his desk reading the evening paper. He switches a small transistor radio on and we hear a blast of pop music. He changes the wavelength—preferably by push button wave-change—and we hear something very radio three: musique concrete or Gregorian chant.* WATT *changes the wavelength again and we hear a well-loved carol. He sticks it for a couple of lines then switches off and goes back to his paper.*

THE HOTEL BALLROOM Night

WILSON *rejoins* MURIEL *at the table, during a lull in the dancing.*

2 WILSON. Any ... exciting new friends?

3 MURIEL. There's time yet.

4 WILSON. I have just met the Lord Lieutenant of the County coming out of the Gentlemen's lavatory.

Quick reaction from MURIEL.

And his friend who's something in Whitehall.

We see the LORD LIEUTENANT'S PARTY *coming into the ballroom and settling at a table.*

5 MURIEL. And their wives.

6 WILSON. Obviously, I didn't meet them ... but they are here.

7 MURIEL. Yes, they are rather.

They drink a toast.

1 WILSON. Peace and prosperity.

2 MURIEL. You always were ambitious.

They laugh.

3 WILSON. Realistic.

THE SQUAD OFFICE Night

WATT opens a drawer and brings out two glasses. Then from his raincoat pocket a small bottle of Scotch. He pours out two modest drinks. Picks up one.

4 WATT [*quietly*]. Compliments of the season. [*He drains the first glass and picks up the second.*] Thanks John. The same to you [*He drains the second.*] Good health. [*He tidies the bottle and glasses away then gets on with some work.*]

THE HOTEL CORRIDOR Night

We are on a different floor. The corridor is deserted. WILSON emerges from one of the rooms carrying a bulging pillowcase. MURIEL comes out with him and sets off walking about six yards in front of him. She approaches a corner, a kind of T-junction, and gives a quick wave of her hand. WILSON drops the bundle so that it looks like part of the day-to-day running—a bundle of laundry awaiting attention. WILSON strolls back casually the way he has just come, away from the bundle. We then see the source of MURIEL's concern—a COUPLE, swaying their way to or from the ballroom. They make their happy way out of harm's way, there is another signal from MURIEL, WILSON picks up his bundle and they're off again. No panic—a smooth professional operation.

THE SQUAD OFFICE Night

WATT is working. The telephone rings.

5 WATT. Double two double four . . . oh hello, that's a surprise . . . no well, I thought you'd be on your hot chestnuts and brown ale . . . I see . . . well, that's a very Christian thought . . . eh? . . . I was pondering setting up some sort

of pagan orgy in the office but . . . [*He looks round the office.*]
. . . I couldn't get a band at such short notice . . . no . . .
very quiet . . .

THE HOTEL CORRIDOR   Night

We see MURIEL *and* WILSON *at the doorway of their bedroom.*
WILSON *swiftly hands over the loaded pillowcase to* MURIEL *and*
continues on along the corridor—as neatly done as a transfer by a
practised relay runner. WILSON *disappears round a corner,* MURIEL
enters the room and closes the door behind her. In this, as in all other
corridor sequences, we can hear the distant sounds of festive jollity.

THE EXTERIOR OF THE HOTEL   Night

A shadowy figure walks round the side of the hotel. We come closer
to the man whom we now identify as WILSON. *He stops beside his car,*
the Rover 3.5 we saw earlier, and whistles lightly. A first floor
window opens quickly and quietly and MURIEL *throws down two or*
three bulging kit-bags. WILSON *picks them up and puts them in the*
car boot, locking the boot and walking away—the whole process, start
to finish, taking place very quickly. He walks round to the front of the
hotel, lighting a cigarette, just like a man who's popped outside for a
smoke—no attempt at concealment but no bravado either—just simple
and well-founded self-confidence.

THE HOTEL BALLROOM   Night.

The dance in full swing, perhaps a few gins noisier, and less inhibited
than before. After a glimpse at the LORD LIEUTENANT'S PARTY,
happy but still conscious of their position in the order of things, we
find the WILSONS *dancing.*

2 WILSON [*mocking*]. Happy, my darling?

3 MURIEL. Oh, if only this evening could go on for ever . . .

   They laugh, obviously an old private joke, then a pause.

   About now do you think?

4 WILSON. About now.

   A pause, then MURIEL *suddenly goes into the first stages of a fainting fit, stumbling against a nearby couple. An amiably bour-geois middle-aged man and wife called* PAYNE.

1 MURIEL. I'm sorry.

2 PAYNE. Are you all right?

3 MURIEL. Just a bit faint . . . it's stupid . . .

4 WILSON. It's the heat in here . . .

5 MRS PAYNE. It's terribly stuffy, I said that last year. I've got some smelling salts in my bag . . .

6 WILSON. I wouldn't care, she's hardly had a drop all night . . .

7 MRS PAYNE. Would you like some smelling salts, dear?

8 MURIEL. I'd prefer fresh air, I think . . .

9 WILSON. Thank you so much but . . .

10 PAYNE. Anything we can do . . .

WILSON *and* MURIEL *make their way to the edge of the dance floor, half-pursued by the* PAYNES.

11 WILSON. I think we can manage, thank you . . .

12 MURIEL. Must be something they put in the beer . . .

13 WILSON. You haven't touched a drop, remember? I told the people.

Everybody admires their brave joking in difficult circumstances.

14 PAYNE. Anything we can do . . .

15 WILSON. We'll meet up later on, have a drink on it . . .

The WILSONS *exit.*

16 MRS PAYNE. What a pity.

17 PAYNE. Yes.

18 MRS PAYNE. Spoiling the party, and nice people, too . . .

19 PAYNE. Very nice, yes.

THE HOTEL CAR PARK Night

A quick, sharp sequence panning with the Rover 3.5 as it accelerates out of the car park, not loud but pretty fast.

THE HOTEL CORRIDOR   Night

We see YVONNE *removing the key from behind the fire extinguisher, slipping it into the pocket of her overall and moving quickly on.*

THE SQUAD OFFICE   Night

WATT *stops working, looks at his watch, switches on his radio. We hear Big Ben sounding . . . it is Christmas Day.*

THE HOTEL BALLROOM   Night

Everybody silently listening to Big Ben, which is being relayed into the ballroom. The chimes cease and there is a burst of cheering and applause and kissing and festive greetings.

THE SQUAD OFFICE   Night

WATT *switches off the radio. He opens his briefcase and takes out three envelopes which he opens. They contain his Christmas cards. He opens them, knowing pretty accurately in advance who they're from. He sets them out on the desk.*

THE BALLROOM   Night

The WILSONS *are now sharing a table with the* PAYNES.

1   MRS PAYNE [*to her husband*]. She's looking much better isn't she?

2   WILSON. And you must join us in celebrating the fact . . .

3   PAYNE. Thank you . . .

4   WILSON. That's if you like champagne . . .

5   PAYNE. I'll struggle through, I daresay . . .

6   MRS PAYNE. You're very kind . . .

7   WILSON. I'm known for my kindness throughout the West country . . . [*He pours out the champagne.*]

8   MURIEL. Do you think I should?

9   WILSON. Kill or cure..

10   MRS PAYNE. I *am* enjoying myself.

They are delighted that such a handsome charming couple as the Wilsons have chosen them as companions.

59

THE SQUAD OFFICE   Night

WATT *packing up some things on his desk—preparing to leave.*

THE BALLROOM   Night

1 PAYNE. All the very best.

2 MURIEL. And to both of you.

3 MRS PAYNE. Merry Christmas . . .

4 PAYNE. And a Happy New Year.

5 WILSON. Good health.

6 MURIEL. Peace and prosperity.

They drink to all of this.

THE SQUAD OFFICE   Night

WATT *has his hat and coat on and is already half-way out of the office when the telephone rings—the extension line from the local station. He hesitates for a moment before coming back to answer it.*

7 WATT. Regional Crime Squad . . . Chief Inspector Watt . . . hello . . . yes . . . where? . . . the Pentland Grange? . . . could have been worse, could have been Buckingham Palace . . . you don't know how much . . . a lot . . . yes, I'm er . . . technically available . . . as it were, yes . . .

THE HOTEL FOYER   Night

A scene of agitation with much coming and going. We see the WILSONS *and the* PAYNES *coming out of the ballroom. And in the background, the* LORD LIEUTENANT *giving the manager of the hotel,* JEFFREYS, *the rough edge of his tongue.*

8 PAYNE. We'll have to check . . .

9 WILSON. We must do the same . . .

10 MRS PAYNE. Isn't it awful . . .

11 MURIEL. Not that we've got anything worth pinching. . .

12 WILSON. Don't be modest dear . . .

1 PAYNE. It's a good job we've got a sense of humour . . .

It's not clear whether MRS PAYNE *shares this sentiment.*

2 WILSON. We shouldn't really be fussing about material possessions, at Christmas of all times . . .

They make their way to their rooms.

THE HOTEL CAR PARK   Night

The squad car drives up to the main entrance. WATT *gets out of the car and goes into the hotel.*

THE HOTEL FOYER   Night

It is quieter now. A few residents are gathered round DETECTIVE SERGEANT CONWAY *of divisional C.I.D., presumably giving details of stolen property.* WATT *is met by* DETECTIVE CONSTABLE RANKIN, *also of divisional C.I.D. He is clearly expecting* WATT.

3 WATT. Detective Chief Inspector Watt, Regional Crime Squad . . .

4 RANKIN. Detective Constable Rankin, Divisional C.I.D. . . .

5 WATT. Who else have you got here?

6 RANKIN. Detective Sergeant Conway . . . he's getting details of the stolen property sir . . .

7 WATT. Good.

8 RANKIN. And there's a squad car outside . . .

9 WATT. Doing what?

10 RANKIN. Maintaining observation sir, in case anybody wants to leave in a hurry.

11 WATT. And a nice warm office with two telephones?

12 RANKIN. This way, sir . . .

RANKIN leads WATT *into the hotel manager's office, a small office leading off the area behind the reception desk.* WATT *smiles at the* RECEPTIONIST.

13 WATT. Good morning.

THE MANAGER'S OFFICE Night

JEFFREYS, *the manager, gets up from his desk as* WATT *and* RANKIN *come in. He is in his forties, smooth and efficient, not without the smarm of his trade. The office is quite small, with two telephones on the desk, and notebooks and pens to hand.*

1 RANKIN. Detective Chief Inspector Watt ... Mr Jeffreys, the Manager ...

2 WATT. Good morning, Mr Jeffreys ...

3 JEFFREYS. Good morning, Inspector.

4 WATT. I'd better not say Merry Christmas ...

5 JEFFREYS. Perhaps not. Please make yourself at home ...

6 WATT. Thank you. I take it most of your guests are in bed?

7 JEFFREYS. Yes.

8 RANKIN. They were all asked to check their rooms for anything missing ...

9 WATT. And Sergeant Conway's getting all the details, good ... [*He looks at the telephones.*] Are these both live?

10 RANKIN. They're connected to a switchboard but I've switched them through ...

11 WATT. So I can move in straight away?

12 JEFFREYS. Everything's at your disposal.

13 WATT. Two things I'd like, Mr Jeffreys ... your hotel register and a list of your staff ...

14 JEFFREYS. That's fairly simple ...

15 WATT. And in the case of the staff, how long each of them has been with you ...

16 JEFFREYS. I'll see to that.

17 WATT. And then we'll let you get some sleep ...

18 JEFFREYS. I'm not sure I'll sleep.

19 WATT. You'll have a trying day ahead ... maintaining the festive spirit in difficult circumstances.

20 JEFFREYS. It's never easy at the best of times.

JEFFREYS goes out, crossing with SERGEANT CONWAY *in the door-way.*

1 WATT. Detective Sergeant Conway . . .

2 CONWAY. Sir.

3 WATT. Detective Chief Inspector Watt . . . completed your list?

4 CONWAY. This seems to be it.

5 WATT. Tell me.

6 CONWAY. Six fur coats . . . two of them around the three thousand mark . . . the others between ten and fifteen hundred pounds . . . a few small amounts in cash, just over a hundred pounds . . . some of them aren't quite sure how much money they had . . .

7 WATT. Must be difficult for them.

8 CONWAY. One or two small items of jewellery . . . about three hundred pounds total . . . overall about eleven thousand pounds' worth . . .

9 WATT. They came upon the midnight clear.

10 CONWAY. The Lord Lieutenant of the County is staying here . . . his party includes a Parliamentary Private Secretary for something or other . . .

11 WATT. Whitewashing coal, probably . . .

12 CONWAY. Both their wives lost their fur coats . . .

13 WATT. That might explain why I was rung up by the Chief Constable himself. *And* why they've called on the Crime Squad . . . everybody up! I take it they're not very happy about losing their coats?

14 CONWAY. Not very. They've been coming here for years, and it's never happened before.

15 WATT. That little girl on the reception desk, does she type?

16 RANKIN. I don't know sir.

17 WATT. Would you like to ask her? And if she says yes, it'll save either of you wasting your time typing this lot out . . . [*He hands the list to* RANKIN.]

18 RANKIN. And then circulated?

1 WATT. Naturally.

    JEFFREYS *comes in with the hotel register and staff list.* RANKIN *goes out.*

2 JEFFREYS. The guests and the staff, Inspector . . .

3 WATT. Thank you.

4 JEFFREYS. Anything else?

5 WATT. I should go to bed if I were you.

6 JEFFREYS. It's a pleasant thought.

7 WATT. I reserve the right to wake you up if we think of anything else.

    JEFFREYS *nods, but does not smile as he goes out.* WATT *and* CONWAY *start a preliminary check through the lists.*

    Looks like a good class of customer.

8 CONWAY. Well, at the price they charge . . .

9 WATT. What's your first name?

10 CONWAY. Reg.

11 WATT. Might as well cut out the formalities . . . we're going to be here some time . . .

    It suddenly becomes clear that WATT *is counting the names.*

    Eighty-seven guests, all to be vetted, plus individual statements from them all . . .

12 CONWAY. And the staff.

13 WATT. I suppose we can eliminate the Lord Lieutenant's party . . . even as accessories . . .

14 CONWAY. If we say ten minutes to take each statement, the answer still comes to . . .

15 WATT. Comes to something bloody ridiculous . . . you a family man?

16 CONWAY. Yes sir.

17 WATT. What time do kids wake up on Christmas morning to open their presents?

18 CONWAY. Six o'clock, seven if you're lucky.

1 WATT [*looking at his watch*]. Ten past four. [*Pause.*] Hard luck, Daddy, you're going to miss it. [*He picks up the telephone.*]

THE HALLWAY OF MORGAN'S HOUSE   Night

The telephone rings, and rings. Eventually MORGAN *comes downstairs in a dressing-gown and answers the telephone, predicting his arrival by switching on the light from a two-way switch on the landing.*

2 MORGAN [*into phone*]. Hello ... oh hello, yes, speaking ... the where? ... Pentland Grange, yes I know ... well ... say half an hour ... that's all right, when duty calls ... half an hour.

MORGAN *puts the telephone down, not happy. Looks upstairs with mingled annoyance and guilt. We hear a child's voice.*

3 CHILD. Daddy ...

THE MANAGER'S OFFICE   Night

4 WATT [*putting the telephone down*]. How to make friends and influence people ... [*He looks again at his watch.*] We can start questioning the staff from about six o'clock, the residents from when, breakfast time I suppose ...

5 CONWAY. Not before eight or nine I should think ...

6 WATT. Mid-day in some cases.

7 CONWAY. They might want to open their presents.

8 WATT. People that stay in hotels for Christmas don't get many presents ... like people that work at Christmas ... now here's a good steady job for you ...

9 CONWAY. Sir.

10 WATT. We're fairly certain how the job was done ... somebody knows exactly which rooms are worth doing ... they get a pass key ... they know what they're after and they get it ... quietly, no fuss ... either they're residents or staff, or outsiders working with somebody inside ... do we agree?

11 CONWAY. A good professional job.

1 WATT. Meaning they've done it before ... I'd like you to find out where and when ...

2 CONWAY. From records?

3 WATT. Start locally then work outwards in ever increasing circles if you'll forgive the expression.

4 CONWAY. Civilian staff at Criminal Records, they'll all be off.

5 WATT. They have homes with telephone numbers ... I said it was a good steady job ...

6 CONWAY. I can imagine some of the replies we'll get.

7 WATT. If they don't like it, they shouldn't join ...

8 CONWAY. It's just having to ask them ...

9 WATT. And if you don't like it, the same applies ... [*He gets up.*] I'm going to have a look round. See how I'd do it. [*He goes out.*]

10 CONWAY [*on telephone*]. Hello, I want Criminal Records please ... I'd like somebody's home number please ... yes, it's Christmas here as well ...

THE HOTEL FOYER   Night

WATT *comes out from the manager's office, as the receptionist,* BRENDA, *finishes typing the list of stolen property—several copies— and gives these to* RANKIN, *who takes them into the manager's office.*

11 WATT. What time do you go home, love?

12 BRENDA. I'm on from six o'clock till midnight ...

13 WATT. I hope you're on overtime.

14 BRENDA. I was just going when the fun started ... so I thought I'd better stay on ... in case I could be useful ... the telephone was red hot ...

15 WATT. You were here all evening?

16 BRENDA. Yes.

17 WATT. Was there very much coming and going?

18 BRENDA. Rather a lot.

19 WATT. Why?

1 BRENDA. It was a nice night. You get people . . . well, Christmas and all that, they decide they want to go and look at the stars, things like that . . .

2 WATT. Funny people.

3 BRENDA. Or else they need fresh air to sober them up . . . it all goes on . . .

4 WATT. So of all the eighty-seven people staying here . . . how many went in and out of that door during the evening?

5 BRENDA. It seemed like . . . hundreds.

6 WATT. Thank you.

7 BRENDA. Was that the right answer?

8 WATT. Not what I wanted to hear but if it's the truth we'll have to live with it.

9 BRENDA. It's the truth.

   Pause.

10 WATT. Pity. [*Looks at his watch.*] The management should send you home.

11 BRENDA. I'm all right.

12 WATT. You need some sleep. It's getting early.

   WATT *goes out through the main doors.*

   OUTSIDE THE HOTEL Night

   WATT *walks round the outside of the hotel getting the lie of the land. He looks up at the bedrooms then at the ground below for signs of criminal activity—nothing specific—just getting the smell of the place.*

   THE MANAGER'S OFFICE Night

   CONWAY *and* RANKIN *having simultaneous telephone conversations —compared with the previous scene, it is all hell let loose.*

13 CONWAY. No signs of forcible entry at all . . .

14 RANKIN. Pentland Grange . . . yes, Grange, G.R.A.N.G.E. . . .

1　CONWAY. Six fur coats ranging in value from one thousand to three thousand pounds approximately . . .

2　RANKIN. Property to the total value of eleven thousand pounds . . . eleven thousand . . .

3　CONWAY. Plus jewellery and a bit of loose change . . .

4　RANKIN. I can't help it if it's a bad line . . . [*to* CONWAY] God give me patience . . .

5　CONWAY. Yes, exactly . . . any similar jobs within the last five years or so . . . soon as you can . . .

6　RANKIN. I said Pentland Grange . . .

7　CONWAY. Smashing. Thanks a lot.

CONWAY *puts the telephone down. Obviously his man was helpful and co-operative. Obviously* RANKIN's *man is not.*

8　RANKIN. Just fetching his pencil . . . Scotsman, I've shot 'em . . . [*on phone again*] Yes . . .?

CONWAY *is about to dial when his telephone rings.*

9　CONWAY. Pentland Grange Hotel. Detective Sergeant Conway . . .

10　RANKIN. Pentland . . . P.E.N.T.L.A.N.D. . . .

THE HOTEL FOYER　Night

WATT *comes in with* MORGAN.

11　MORGAN. Saw you wandering about and . . .

12　WATT. Loitering, you thought.

13　MORGAN. Crossed my mind, yes. Till I recognized you.

14　WATT. Couple of uniformed lads thought they had me as well.

15　MORGAN. Anything to see?

16　WATT. Windows to drop things from . . . ground for it to fall on . . . but I could have guessed all that. I wanted to be sure the uniformed lads were awake. [*Afterthought.*] Sorry I spoiled your Christmas. This way.

WATT *leads* MORGAN *into the office.*

THE MANAGER'S OFFICE Night

CONWAY *is on the phone taking down details from a caller at the other end.*

1 WATT. Any joy?

2 RANKIN. A little bit.

3 WATT. Good. Share it with Detective Constable Morgan of the Crime Squad . . .

4 CONWAY. Thank you, we'll be in touch later. [*He puts the phone down.*]

5 WATT. Detective Sergeant Conway, D.C. Rankin . . . tidings of great joy . . . ?

6 RANKIN. According to C.R.O. Glasgow, this job's like one last Christmas at St Andrew's. And Lancro had one the same the year before at Keswick . . .

7 WATT. Lake District?

8 RANKIN. Yes. *And* one booked by West Riding the year before that, at Matlock in Derbyshire . . .

9 WATT. Good. What are the points of resemblance?

10 RANKIN. Christmas holiday season . . . expensive hotels . . . fur coats . . . concentrating on a dozen rooms . . . access to a master key . . .

11 MORGAN. How do they know which rooms to choose?

12 WATT. They sit in the foyer and watch the guests arrive, select the victims . . .

13 MORGAN. Unless it's somebody on the staff . . .

14 WATT. We need to know the names of the staff and guests at these other hotels . . . have they got them?

15 RANKIN. Apparently yes. They're sending them through by teleprinter . . .

16 WATT. Where to?

17 RANKIN. I told them Divisional H.Q.

WATT *sorts through the various sheets of information.*

1 WATT. You two . . . [*to* RANKIN *and* CONWAY] . . . I want you to go through these lists, everybody that's staying or working here . . . I want them cleared . . . I want to know they're honest in the eyes of the law . . .

2 CONWAY. Or not as the case may be . . .

3 WATT. Check their addresses, see they really do live there . . .

4 MORGAN. And what do we do?

5 WATT. We do the frontal approach . . . to their faces . . .

6 MORGAN. Right.

7 WATT. You'd better read these first . . . description of the property . . . and a few initial statements . . . [*He looks at his watch again.*] They'll be emerging from their drunken stupors before long.

8 MORGAN [*looking up from his reading*]. To see if Santa Claus has been . . .

9 CONWAY. He's been. With an empty sack . . .

10 WATT [*at window*]. Dawn's breaking. Hope that's some sort of omen.

OUTSIDE THE HOTEL Day

A dawn shot through the trees then panning down to a scene of quiet, purposeful activity as the POLICE *search the grounds. A sequence of shots so that we see the component parts of the search. A* DOG-HANDLER *with his* DOG *searching the undergrowth: one or two* MEN *opening the boots of cars and looking round inside: a* FORENSIC EXPERT *checking for fingerprints on windows.*

THE HOTEL DINING-ROOM Day.

Not another set but merely the reverse side of the swing doors between dining-room and kitchen. YVONNE BALL *carries a tray of dirty dishes through the swing doors into the kitchen. We hear the sounds of breakfast being prepared.*

THE HOTEL KITCHEN Day

WATT *is waiting inside the kitchen for* YVONNE. WATT *is in quite a flippant mood.*

1 WATT. And the next little lady . . .

2 YVONNE. I beg your pardon . . .

3 WATT. If you could spare a minute. I'd like to solve a serious crime . . .

4 YVONNE. There's people waiting for their breakfast . . .

5 WATT. I'm waiting for mine as well . . .

6 YVONNE. Long as you square it with the management . . .

7 WATT. I'll fix them.

They move to one side, out of the immediate rush.

Now, I thought I'd spoken to all the kitchen staff . . .

8 YVONNE. You tell me.

9 WATT. Miss Yvonne Ball . . .

10 YVONNE. That's right . . .

11 WATT. You're down here as a chambermaid . . .

12 YVONNE. Working a bit extra over Christmas, help them over the rush . . .

13 WATT. Very loyal.

14 YVONNE. I just need the money.

15 WATT. Where were you last night?

16 YVONNE. Well, all over really . . .

17 WATT. Can you be more precise?

18 YVONNE. I was helping in here, in the kitchens, till nine o'clock, then I went up to my room listened to the radio, went to bed about eleven, I suppose . . .

19 WATT. Did you leave your room at all?

20 YVONNE. Maybe twice . . .

21 WATT. What for?

22 YVONNE [*as to a child*]. To leave the room . . .

23 WATT. Did you see anything unusual at all last night, at any time, anybody behaving out of the ordinary . . .

24 YVONNE. They all go a bit mad on Christmas Eve . . . I mean I keep out of the way . . .

1 WATT. Why?

2 YVONNE. Old men . . . thinking they're twenty-one again.

3 WATT. Don't they bring their wives?

4 YVONNE. They're usually swimming in gin . . . I thought we were investigating a serious crime.

5 WATT. You started here in November . . .

6 YVONNE. That's right.

7 WATT. Where were you before then?

8 YVONNE. Having a baby.

9 WATT. I . . . see . . .

10 YVONNE. But no feller, you see. So I need the money. So I work long hours. People. Breakfast, you know.

11 WATT. I find it very difficult to forget breakfast, love. You're on bedrooms so you have access to a pass key.

12 YVONNE. Well it's central heating so you can't go down the chimneys.

13 WATT. Not even at Christmas.

14 YVONNE. Not even at Christmas.

15 WATT. You have a key.

16 YVONNE. Yes.

17 WATT. Does it ever leave your possession?

18 YVONNE. No.

19 WATT. Never?

20 YVONNE. Only when I lend it to anybody that wants to steal things from the rooms . . . [*Pause.*] You can't take a baby in prison.

21 WATT. Who looks after the baby?

22 YVONNE. My mother. But I have to give her the money, she's got none . . . she hasn't got a feller either . . .

WATT *raises an eyebrow.*

My dad was lost at sea.

23 WATT. Sorry.

1 YVONNE. And that's why I work long hours or did I mention it?

WATT *can't help liking her.*

2 WATT. I'm not sure I blame those old men . . .

3 YVONNE. Oh my word, I'd better get back to work . . .

4 WATT. Aye, get on, the poached eggs'll be all soggy.

5 YVONNE. Hey . . .

6 WATT. What?

7 YVONNE. Do you fancy a bacon sandwich?

8 WATT. At least.

YVONNE *giggles and goes off into the kitchen. Another* WAITRESS *comes in.*

Can you spare a minute? We're nearly through.

THE MANAGER'S OFFICE   Day

9 CONWAY. Well, that's cleared everybody on the staff.

10 RANKIN. All of them?

11 CONWAY. Not a stain on their characters . . .

12 RANKIN. Officially.

13 CONWAY. In the eyes of the law. They might be a set of villains yes . . . What about the guests?

14 RANKIN. Half-way through . . . they're not just honest, they're flaming dull . . .

THE HOTEL FOYER   Day

MORGAN *is talking to* MR *and* MRS PAYNE *in the lounge part of the foyer. He is finding them rather dull.*

15 MORGAN. Did you leave the dance at any time to go outside?

16 PAYNE. No, we didn't go outside.

17 MORGAN. Or upstairs?

18 MRS PAYNE. No.

73

1 PAYNE. We didn't go upstairs until the other people found their things were missing, so we went to check . . . of course, they hadn't touched our room . . .

2 MRS PAYNE. I do *have* a fur coat but not the sort anybody would be likely to steal . . . [*She smiles but a shade too self-consciously.*]

3 PAYNE. And I always keep my cash on me . . . never leave it lying around . . .

4 MORGAN. Do you remember anything unusual happening?

5 PAYNE. Not really.

6 MRS PAYNE. Mrs Wilson felt faint, that's all . . .

7 MORGAN. Mrs Wilson? [*He checks his list.*]

8 MRS PAYNE. Yes.

9 PAYNE. I don't suppose it's important.

10 MORGAN. Mr and Mrs Charles Wilson.

11 PAYNE. That's right. Charles and Muriel . . .

12 MRS PAYNE. Muriel, yes, she felt faint during the dance, so the two of them went outside for some fresh air.

13 MORGAN. They're friends of yours?

14 PAYNE. Well, only since last night . . . very charming people . . .

15 MRS PAYNE. A lovely couple.

16 MORGAN. What time did they go outside?

17 PAYNE. About . . . half past eleven, something like that . . .

18 MORGAN. Were they away long?

19 PAYNE. Half an hour maybe . . .

20 MRS PAYNE. Less.

21 PAYNE. Are you sure?

22 MRS PAYNE. They were back before midnight, we toasted Christmas . . .

23 PAYNE. That's right . . .

24 MRS PAYNE. We had champagne and Big Ben and everything . . .

1   MORGAN. Must have been very nice . . .

2   MRS PAYNE. Oh and you'll be missing your Christmas, won't you, what a shame, will you get your dinner?

3   MORGAN. I haven't the slightest idea, Mrs Payne . . .

4   PAYNE. Anyway, if Charles and Muriel saw anything, I'm sure they'll tell you about it . . .

5   MRS PAYNE. Oh yes, they'll be good witnesses, is that what you call it? Lovely people.

THE MANAGER'S OFFICE   Day

6   CONWAY [on the phone]. I am very sorry. We've got a dozen and a half men here who'd all rather be with their wives and kids, but it can't be helped . . . if you don't like it, you shouldn't have joined . . . O.K.? . . . so if you could do that . . . I said please . . . thank you very much . . . now! [He slams the phone down.] Am I inconsiderate?

7   RANKIN. Never, Sergeant.

8   CONWAY. Half the time I'm not even sure who I'm talking to . . . [He rummages among the papers to see what he's supposed to be doing next.] Probably find tomorrow I used an obscene expression to the Director of Public Prosecutions. I wonder if we're getting any dinner.

THE BALLROOM   Day

The place is deserted but ready for the day's party to come. WATT is talking to JEFFREYS.

9   WATT. I've got to be blunt about this, Mr Jeffreys . . . are there any members of your hotel staff that you're not happy about?

10 JEFFREYS. Not happy about?

11 WATT. I don't have to spell it out, do I?

12 JEFFREYS. None of them have criminal records, if that's what you mean.

13 WATT. We know they haven't got records, we've checked that.

75

1 JEFFREYS. You're very efficient, Inspector.

2 WATT. I know. I'm asking you something that we can't find out by efficiency ... I'm asking you to read character ... and tell me if you see anything that worries you.

3 JEFFREYS. I read character before I engage them in the first place. I have no comments to make. Certainly no worries.

Pause.

4 WATT. What about the guests?

5 JEFFREYS. How can I answer that?

6 WATT. Don't answer at all if it bothers you.

7 JEFFREYS. What can I say? They're strangers to me, for the most part ... some of them drink too much ... occasionally we discover a man and his wife who aren't what they seem ... the John Smith syndrome ... but there are no habitual criminals in this hotel as far as I am aware.

8 WATT. Good.

9 JEFFREYS. It's ridiculous to suggest such a thing.

10 WATT. I hope we don't end up looking ridiculous.

THE MANAGER'S OFFICE   Day

11 CONWAY [*on the phone*]. Yes, four people from the Birmingham area we'd like clearing ... Mr and Mrs Charles Wilson, Flat 4, Warwick Gardens, Birmingham ... and Mr and Mrs Albert Neal, 44 Stansdale Road ... thank you. Soon as possible. And the same to you.

THE HOTEL FOYER   Day

12 BRENDA. Can you take this call?

13 MORGAN. Hasn't it gone to the office?

14 BRENDA. Both their lines are engaged ...

MORGAN *takes the call.*

15 MORGAN. Hello, D.C. Morgan ... oh, hello sir ... just a moment, I think I ... [*as* WATT *walks up*] Mr Barlow for you.

1   WATT. Just what I wanted.

We need only see the corner where the phone is. BARLOW *is wearing a funny hat, smoking a cigar, possibly with a glass in his hand, and is very jovial. Continue intercutting between* BARLOW *and* WATT *as required.*

2   WATT. Hello sir.

3   BARLOW. How's it going, John?

4   WATT. Well enough . . . it's all information, from all directions, just waiting for things to start overlapping.

5   BARLOW. Do you need any help?

6   WATT. No, I think everything's under control.

7   BARLOW. I'd be happy to pop in. I'm just killing time really.

8   WATT. Thank you for the offer. I'll keep the option open.

9   BARLOW. Don't lose too much sleep over it.

10 WATT. Thanks for ringing.

THE HOTEL FOYER   Day

11 WATT. Mr Barlow . . . how's it going keep up the good work, you know . . .

12 MORGAN. I couldn't help hearing, sir, even from here . . .

13 WATT. I'm always hearing his voice, even when it isn't there . . . you didn't hear me say that, Morgan . . . come on . . . [*He leads* MORGAN *into the office.*]

THE MANAGER'S OFFICE   Day

WATT *and* MORGAN *come in.* CONWAY, *inevitably, is on the telephone.* RANKIN *is checking lists.*

14 CONWAY. O.K. thanks a lot . . . you can't win them all . . .

He puts the phone down and is about to dial a new number when WATT *restrains him.*

1   WATT. Hang on, let's take a deep breath. [*He lights a cigarette.*] Right. Anything on the search?

2   CONWAY. Nothing sir. Inside or outside.

3   WATT. Anything more about those other hotel jobs?

4   RANKIN. Confirmation about the method . . . access to the rooms . . . and all the stuff away sharp . . .

5   WATT. Lists of names?

6   RANKIN. Not yet.

7   WATT. Have to start screaming at them soon . . .

8   RANKIN. Criminal Record Offices are having to contact local C.I.D. in all the areas . . .

9   WATT. It's their job.

10   CONWAY. Anything from the staff, sir?

11   WATT. I've talked to them all. They've all got good stories. One or two feelings, no evidence . . .

There is a knock at the door.

Come in . . .

The RECEPTIONIST *comes in.*

12   BRENDA. The Lord Lieutenant would like a word . . .

13   WATT. I daresay . . . [*Pause.*] All right.

WATT *goes out with the* RECEPTIONIST.

14   CONWAY. I bet I know what the word is.

15   RANKIN. Have you found any villains among the guests?

16   MORGAN. Talked to about half of them . . . they all seem very respectable . . . there's a few people who left the dance between ten o'clock and midnight . . . for various reasons . . .

17   CONWAY. I can imagine . . .

18   RANKIN. How many?

19   MORGAN. Getting on for twenty.

20   CONWAY. It's a help.

1   MORGAN. It's difficult though. Hardly any of them were sober at the time, it seems.

2   RANKIN. Except the one that did the job.

3   CONWAY [*looking at* MORGAN'S *notes*]. You've done well to get this far.

    WATT *comes in.*

4   WATT. The noble Lord presents his compliments, a solicitous inquiry about how we're getting on and respectfully requests fingers out . . .

5   CONWAY. I was going to suggest we help D.C. Morgan with his talking to the guests, sir . . . still a lot to do and . . .

6   WATT. Are you top side of your telephoning?

7   CONWAY. Mainly incoming now . . .

8   WATT. O.K. I'll be telephone girl for a while . . . change of air all round, off you go . . .

    MORGAN, RANKIN *and* CONWAY *go out.* WATT *sits down and relaxes for a moment. He takes a deep breath and plunges into the lists again. A knock at the door.*

    Come in.

    JONES *comes in.*

9   JONES. Compliments of the season, John.

10 WATT. Yes, that makes me feel a lot better . . .

    JONES *has two glasses in his hand and brings out a bottle from his coat.*

11 JONES. Does that help?

12 WATT. It's practical.

    JONES *pours out a couple of drinks.*

13 JONES. I came by way of Division . . . that's why the bottle isn't full . . . they'd just got these in on the teleprinter, they looked relevant, so . . . [*He hands* WATT *the guest lists from the other jobs.*]

14 WATT. They are.

1 JONES. Looked to me like lists of names.

2 WATT. Sharp observation.

3 JONES. I'm noted for it.

They browse through the lists.

4 WATT. Four Christmases on the trot, four hotel jobs . . . near as dammit identical . . .

5 JONES. You don't suppose the thieves use the same names every time?

6 WATT. Highly unlikely.

7 JONES. But the initials . . .?

8 WATT. There's over a hundred and fifty names on each list . . . how long are you staying Arthur?

9 JONES. Ten minutes. Just popped in . . . Christmas cheer . . .

10 WATT. That was your first mistake . . .

WATT gives JONES two of the lists to check.

11 JONES. Yes, I think it was.

There is a knock on the door.

12 WATT. Come in.

YVONNE comes in with a tray, on it are coffee and sandwiches.

13 YVONNE. You missed your Christmas dinner . . .

14 WATT. It had crossed my mind . . . so I whispered to the manager . . .

15 YVONNE. It got through . . . turkey sandwiches all right?

16 WATT. Fine thanks.

17 JONES. I had mine before I came out.

18 WATT. But you'll force yourself to have some coffee . . .

19 JONES. I daresay . . .

20 WATT. Thanks very much, love. You'll get your reward in Heaven.

21 YVONNE. If I live that long. [*She goes out.*]

1   WATT. Well?

2   JONES. Thank you very much Arthur Jones, for giving up his Christmas Day to help . . .

3   WATT. Thanks Arthur . . . cheers . . . [*He toasts him with a turkey sandwich.*] I wonder who'll thank me?

THE HOTEL FOYER   Day

In the lounge area. MORGAN *is talking to the* WILSONS. *They are in mid-interview.*

4   MORGAN. And you had a fainting fit?

5   MURIEL. How did you know about that?

6   MORGAN. One of your friends mentioned it . . .

7   WILSON. Mr and Mrs Payne?

8   MORGAN. It might have been, I'd have to check back . . .

9   WILSON. The fabulous Paynes . . . [*He regards the* PAYNES *with a good-natured tolerance.*]

10 MORGAN. Are you feeling all right now?

11 MURIEL. Fine, thank you.

12 WILSON. Anyway, I'm sorry we can't be more helpful . . . as I say, we did go outside but we were rather preoccupied with the fainting and fresh air and so on . . .

13 MORGAN. And you saw nothing.

14 MURIEL. I had my head between my knees, I hope that isn't rude . . .

They laugh.

15 MORGAN [*looking at his list*]. You had something stolen, I see.

16 MURIEL. A ring . . . yes.

17 WILSON. Nothing very exotic. And it was insured. You must be feeling the strain. Would you like a drink?

The WILSONS *are drinking—modestly.*

18 MORGAN. I'd love one but I'm at work.

19 WILSON. Terrible dilemma.

1 MORGAN. I suppose so.

2 WILSON. But it's all a bit like that, isn't it?

3 MORGAN. I'm sorry?

4 WILSON. A dilemma . . . I mean all you lads carrying out your investigations, on Christmas Day of all days . . . and on whose behalf?

5 MORGAN. People who've had valuable property stolen.

6 WILSON. People who can well afford it . . . people who've got everything adequately insured . . .

7 MORGAN. Everybody's equal in the eyes of the law.

8 MURIEL. There's a little girl in the kitchen, been working twelve, fourteen hours a day . . . for all these people . . .

9 MORGAN. Including you . . .

10 WILSON. It all comes down to redistribution of wealth.

11 MORGAN. My father's in the mines, I know all about it.

12 WILSON. So we both believe in it.

13 MORGAN. In what?

14 MURIEL. Redistribution of wealth . . .. it's his favourite theme when he's been drinking . . .

15 WILSON. And sober too . . . [*He is pretty sober in fact.*] And look around . . . we're not doing very well, are we?

16 MORGAN. I guess not.

They look round and they're not.

I've got work to do.

17 WILSON. Sorry . . . we've kept you talking.

18 MORGAN. It's been more interesting than the other five hundred and sixty-nine . . .

MORGAN *gets up and moves away with a smile. He really has enjoyed this conversation more than most.*

19 WILSON. I love the 'little working girl in the kitchen' bit.

20 MURIEL. Dickensian, it's seasonal.

1   WILSON. Well, she's got a couple of hundred to feed the baby, now.

2   MURIEL. She'll be able to move out of the stable next year.

OUTSIDE THE HOTEL   Night

A long shot of the hotel — lights blazing merrily in the dark—zoom in slowly so that we can hear the noise of music and merriment.

THE MANAGER'S OFFICE   Night

The noise increases in volume as WATT *comes into the office to join* JONES. *A drop in volume as he closes the door.*

3   WATT. I read somewhere that it used to be a pagan festival . . .

4   JONES. So?

5   WATT. *Used* to be, it said. [*He sits down and picks up where he left off with the lists.*] Did you ring your wife?

6   JONES. Yes.

7   WATT. What did she say?

A silent look from JONES.

I *am* sorry.

A pause. They work.

8   JONES. Where are the lads?

9   WATT. I sent them down to the kitchen to steal some food for themselves.

10 JONES. The nobility shines out of your soul John.

11 WATT. Only in a bad light.

Pause.

12 JONES. What?

13 WATT. I didn't say anything.

14 JONES. Sorry.

15 WATT. Yes I did . . .

WATT *has found something.*

1 JONES. John . . .

2 WATT. I said Charles and Muriel Wilson.

3 JONES. Funny thing to say.

4 WATT. Look. Last year, at the hotel at St Andrews . . . Charles and Marie Walton . . . 1966 at Keswick, Carl and Maureen Wolfe . . . the year before at Matlock . . . Christopher and Margaret Webster . . .

5 JONES. They're still here?

6 WATT. Yes.

7 JONES. Check it.

THE HOTEL BALLROOM   Night

We see MORGAN *making his way round the side of the ballroom, on the look-out for the* WILSONS *among the guests. There is no sign of them.*

THE MANAGER'S OFFICE   Night

WATT *is taking down some details from criminal records, repeating them for* JONES's *benefit.*

8 WATT. Real name Charles Edward Winters . . . public school education . . . one conviction in 1955 . . . stole a fistful of jewellery from a hotel in Brighton . . . now aged thirty-seven . . . yes . . . description fits . . . you'll send the photograph . . . yes, Crime Squad Wyevern . . . good, many thanks . . . [*He puts the phone down.*] That's our man. Nothing on the woman.

9 JONES. He'll have picked her up on the way.

10 WATT. They're sending the photo by transmitter . . .

11 JONES. Haul them in here and now, put it to them straight . . .

12 WATT. And they'll say . . . 'stolen property? What stolen property?'

13 JONES. So what's the alternative?

14 WATT. Let them lead us to it.

15 JONES. They might not leave till the day after Boxing Day . . .

that's the official time . . . the Lord Lieutenant might run out of patience . . .

2   WATT. He's not the only one. [*He gets up.*] Just give them a nudge, I think.

3   JONES Gently.

4   WATT. I'm not given to impetuosity . . . that's more your Welsh valley products . . . [*He goes out.*]

THE HOTEL BALLROOM   Night

The WILSONS *arriving for the dance which is about to start soon. We are aware of* MORGAN *watching from across the room, and* CONWAY *—not obviously—following the* WILSONS *into the ballroom.*

5   WILSON. Darling you look lovely tonight.

6   MURIEL. So do you, darling.

7   WILSON. I know.

This is an amiable send-up of their fellow guests and of themselves.

8   MURIEL. I suppose this is the real meaning of Christmas . . .

9   WILSON. Getting stoned out of your mind?

10   MURIEL. That sort of thing.

The music finishes. We go with them to their table.

11   WILSON. Where next? Biarritz?

12   MURIEL. I've always fancied Baden–Baden . . .

13   WILSON. I don't even know the man.

They smile and nod their greetings to the PAYNES *as they pass them, then reach their table as* WATT *approaches.*

Good evening . . .

14   WATT. Good evening . . . I'm Detective Chief Inspector Watt . . . Mr and Mrs Wilson?

15   MURIEL. That's right . . .

16   WATT. Mind if I rest my feet at your table? Most other places are full.

17   WILSON. You're very welcome.

They sit down.

Come to survey the decadence?

2 WATT. You find it decadent?

3 WILSON. Wasteful.

4 MURIEL. Pleasant as well . . .

5 WATT. You mean . . . starving children in India, that argument.

6 WILSON. I suppose so.

7 WATT. I agree. [*Pause.*] How does it compare with St Andrews?

8 WILSON. I beg your pardon?

9 WATT. St Andrews . . . it's in Scotland . . . or Keswick . . . or Matlock.

10 MURIEL. Sorry Mr Watt, I'm not really with you . . .

11 WATT. Well we've been working non-stop since God knows when and things start getting . . . I don't know . . . sort of surrealistic . . . let's try this . . . [*He reads from a bit of paper.*] Charles and Marie Walton . . . Carl and Maureen Wolfe . . . Christopher and Margaret Webster . . . have you ever travelled under those names?

12 WILSON. It sounds a highly unlikely thing for anybody to do.

13 WATT. I agree. It's just a coincidence that cropped up, I thought I'd better put it to you, straight . . .

14 MURIEL. I'm afraid my head's spinning . . .

15 WATT. So if I asked for a signed statement to the effect that you've never used these other names . . .

16 WILSON. You may have it . . .

17 WATT. Just a coincidence.

18 WILSON. Just a coincidence.

19 WATT. I thought it must be. [*He gets up.*] If you'll excuse me, I've got a half-finished turkey sandwich below stairs.

   [*He moves away from the table.*]

20 WILSON. Well darling . . .

21 MURIEL. If only tonight could last forever . . .

1 WILSON. If only.

THE MANAGER'S OFFICE Night

2 JONES [*on the telephone*]. Good ... good ... You've made me very happy ... now listen ... nobody is to move the car ... just maintain observation ... discreetly ... and await further instructions ... right? ... good lad ...

JONES *puts the phone down. He gets up and is on his way out to look for* WATT, *who beats him to it and meets him at the door.*

We've got them, John.

3 WATT. Who have we got?

4 JONES. Lonely copper pounding his beat not five miles away, stops to look in a car park, finds a Morris 1100 stolen in Birmingham a week ago ... asks for assistance, they open the boot ...

5 WATT. And it's full of fur coats.

6 JONES. Yes.

7 WATT. And I've just put the frighteners on the Wilsons ...

8 JONES. Gently?

9 WATT. So gently you'd never notice ... but they noticed.

10 JONES. If we watch both ends something's bound to happen.

THE HOTEL FOYER Night

WILSON *is at the desk settling his bill.* MURIEL *is nearby and their cases are with a porter, waiting to go out to the car.*

11 WILSON. We don't think it's anything serious, but a kid of seven needs his parents when he's ill ...

12 BRENDA. I hope he's better when you get home.

13 WILSON. Thank you. And I hope *your* troubles are sorted out, too ...

14 BRENDA. It makes life interesting.

15 WILSON. My feeling exactly.

He leaves the desk and goes out with the PORTER *and* MURIEL. WATT *emerges from the manager's office.* WATT *turns to somebody in the office.*

1   WATT. Warn them. They're just leaving.

OUTSIDE THE HOTEL   Night

The Rover 3.5 leaves the car park and drives off down the road. A police car drives out of a side turning and follows in careful and distant pursuit.

THE MANAGER'S OFFICE   Night

JONES *sitting waiting,* WATT *pacing, a pause then the telephone rings.*

2   JONES. Hello . . . yes . . . yes . . . no, no medals . . . you'd have got a rollicking if you'd made a mess of it, that's all . . . [*He puts the phone down.*] We got them.

3   WATT. Any trouble?

4   JONES. They pulled up in the car park, the woman got out of the Rover and into the other car.

5   WATT. The one with the stuff in?

6   JONES. Yes. All ready to set off in convoy . . . and our lads blocked the entrances.

7   WATT. No fighting?

8   JONES [*quietly*]. All peace and goodwill.

9   WATT. Good. [*Pause.*] Merry Christmas, Arthur.

10   JONES. Too late. You've missed it.

THE HOTEL BALLROOM   Night

The guests are singing 'Auld Lang Syne'. Among them we see the PAYNES, *joining in heartily, and the* LORD LIEUTENANT'S PARTY *joining in with sober dignity.*

THE MANAGER'S OFFICE   Night

BARLOW *comes in.*

11   BARLOW. Evening John.

12   WATT. Morning, that should be.

1   BARLOW. On my way home from a party, just popped in and everything's sorted . . .

2   WATT. It took about twenty-four hours . . .

3   BARLOW. I saw the Lord Lieutenant on the way in here . . . he's very grateful to the Squad . . .

4   WATT. He wishes it to be made known . . .

Pause.

5   BARLOW. Who was the inside accomplice, John?

6   WATT. Don't know yet. I was planning to ask them.

7   BARLOW. I should.

A knock at the door.

Come in.

YVONNE *comes in with a tray of coffee.*

8   YVONNE. There's your coffee.

9   WATT. Thanks, love.

10 BARLOW. Got yourself well organized.

11 WATT. It all comes down to organization.

12 YVONNE. You caught them, then?

13 WATT. Yes.

14 YVONNE. It'll seem quiet now. No excitement.

15 WATT. Here . . .

WATT *gives* YVONNE *a pound note.*

Get a present for your baby.

16 YVONNE. Thank you very much. [*She goes out*].

17 BARLOW. Christmas Spirit . . .

18 WATT. I'm right out of gold and frankincense . . . [*He sips his coffee.*] I'll just have my coffee then I'll go down to Divisional H.Q. . . . talk to the Wilsons. Find out who gave them the key.

And a Little Love Besides

A play for the theatre

CHARACTERS

CARTER
MRS HENNESSY
AMY
BRIGGS
MITCHELL
HENNESSY
MRS CARTER
LINDA

INTRODUCTORY NOTE BY ALAN PLATER

This is intended to be a draft script, no more precise and immovable than any other script, at any other stage, i.e. everything is fluid. For this reason there are no 'character notes' because, if a full length play script doesn't give any clues about the people, a paragraph of glib explanation is neither here nor there.

A handful of practical things are known. The setting of the piece, in a literal sense, is the living-room of a vicarage which at times becomes the church itself and at other times the stage of the theatre. All these changes should be achieved by using lighting, sound, acting and physical scene changes. At its simplest, the play could be done with a few assorted chairs and in any case we won't need much more, it won't stand tarting up. Neither will the characters. A few things are self-evident. CARTER is a vicar, his wife a vicar's wife. HENNESSY is a shopkeeper, MRS HENNESSY a shop-keeper's wife. MITCHELL is old enough to have a teenage daughter, BRIGGS is in his early forties, AMY is at school, and LINDA is a doll. Beyond that I don't know much about their faces, figures or even their ages. CARTER could be a young firebrand or a middle-aged academic. The liberals, so-called, could be played militant and loud, or quiet and subdued—similarly with the reactionaries, so-called. And it all depends on your point of view which side is which anyway.

This is simply a plea to avoid easy conclusions and typecasting and playing. Because BRIGGS commits a social misdemeanor, he doesn't have to wear a sensible raincoat and steel-rimmed spectacles, the plain don't have a prerogative of loneliness and anguish. In other words, it's a collective process to be resolved collectively—and we can always alter the script to suit what happens.

And a Little Love Besides

ACT ONE

The lights go up and on stage are CARTER, BRIGGS, MR *and* MRS HENNESSY, MITCHELL *and* AMY. *They are singing with spirit just short of evangelical fervour.*

1 ALL. I will climb the City Wall,
   I will see the Pastures Green,
   I will drink the Nectar Sweet,
   He will make me clean.
   I will climb, I will see,
   I will drink the Nectar.

   I will climb the Mountain Top,
   I will see the Promised Land,
   I will drink the Waters Bright,
   He will touch my hand.
   I will climb, I will see,
   I will drink the Waters.

   I will climb to Calvary,
   I will see the Crosses Three,
   I will drink the Holy Wine,
   He will smile at me.
   I will climb, I will see,
   I will drink the Wine.

   Amen.

2 CARTER. Let us pray.

   Together they say the Lord's Prayer, very quietly, so that we scarcely hear the words: just a gentle murmur ending, predictably, with Amen.

3 CARTER. And now to the real business of the evening . . . if you'd just like to fight for the best seats . . .

   They sit down. The seats have a clear order of precedence, in position and comfort. MR *and* MRS HENNESSY *have the best, followed by*

93

MITCHELL, BRIGGS *and* AMY *in that order. Everybody pretends this is not really the case, but they know.*

1 CARTER. Now in the few weeks since I came to St Amber's I've got very attached to these meetings of the Friday Fellowship ... meeting on Thursday for this week only by the way ... and none more so than tonight when Mr Briggs ...

BRIGGS *stands up, a little self-consciously.*

... is going to tell us what happened on the Youth Club's Easter visit to the Lake District. It would have been nice to see a few of the Youth Club here tonight ...

2 MRS HENNESSY. Here here ...

3 AMY. They're all doing G.C.E.

4 CARTER. And I understand there is a formidable counter-attraction at the Municipal Baths Ballroom ... a psychedelic experience by a new group called ...

CARTER *pauses to think.* AMY *finishes the sentence for him, with respect.*

5 AMY. The Only Begotten and his Flock.

6 CARTER. But thus depleted, and with eager anticipation, I will leave you in Mr Briggs's very capable hands.

BRIGGS, *who is just going to sit down again, walks across to his speaking position.*

7 BRIGGS. Thank you ... I wonder ...?

8 CARTER. Yes?

9 BRIGGS. Would you mind working the projector?

10 CARTER. Delighted. I always believe in having a second trade, in case Christianity falls on hard times.

Uneasy laughter, including a silence from MRS HENNESSY.

11 BRIGGS. Could we have the lights out please?

A pause, then AMY, MITCHELL *and—a beat later—*HENNESSY, *get up. They all hesitate, each waiting for the other.* AMY *sits down,*

94

assuming it's a man's job. HENNESSY *and* MITCHELL *pause, then*
MITCHELL *sits down, assuming* HENNESSY *will go, because he's*
nearer, but HENNESSY *also sits down.* BRIGGS *crosses to the switch*
and does the lights himself.

During the lecture sequence CARTER *is positioned at the front of stage*
working the projector. BRIGGS *is further back lecturing diagonally*
across the stage to his audience. We get a good sight of the slides
throughout. The lighting, subdued, favours BRIGGS *and* CARTER.

1 BRIGGS. Now as most of you know, for the past seventeen
years we've been running Youth Club Easter visits to
the Lake District and this year was no exception. First
slide please.

CARTER *fumbles with the projector, with no visible result.*

We took fourteen young people on the visit, seven boys
and seven ... girls, a good socially balanced number we
thought, in case there were any barn dances ... there
weren't any, if we could have the first slide please ...

CARTER *continues a quiet bit of infighting with the projector as*
BRIGGS *carries on.*

Incidentally I'm sorry I've been so long with this talk
but I still had seven exposures on the film when we got
back and I used them up on the May Day carnival and
just got the prints from Boots on Monday. Can we have
the first one please?

2 CARTER. Get in! That's it.

SLIDE: Railway Silver Band on the march.

3 BRIGGS. Ah. Now. That appears to be ...

4 MITCHELL. Railway Silver Band.

5 BRIGGS. May Day Carnival. My mistake. A 50th at F 11 for
the technically minded ... next please ...

NEXT SLIDE: Out of focus long shot of lake.

Lake Windermere.

Pause.

1 HENNESSY. Is it?

2 BRIGGS. Should be.

3 HENNESSY. Upside down.

4 BRIGGS. Is it?

5 CARTER. Try that.

   CARTER *puts the slide in the other way up.*

6 MRS HENNESSY. It's still upside down.

7 HENNESSY. Looks upside down both ways. Funny.

8 MITCHELL. Overexposed.

9 BRIGGS. A 50th at F 11. Shouldn't be.

10 MITCHELL. Overexposed.

11 HENNESSY. Both ways it looks upside down.

    CARTER *puts the slide in the original way.*

12 BRIGGS. Probably the reflection gives that impression. The very excellent official guide book tells us it was formed originally by . . . glaciation.

    A spot on CARTER *as he addresses the audience.* BRIGGS *continues his lecture silently in the background.*

13 CARTER [*to audience*]. Edward Briggs, pillar of the church. It's free so you don't expect Karsh of Ottawa, or even Karsh of Huddersfield. He was all lined up for the Nobel Prize for Thursday lectures but had to withdraw with a pulled muscle.

14 BRIGGS. Next slide please.

    CARTER'*s attention returns to his work. The next slide is Windermere again.*

    The lake again, with one vital difference.

15 MITCHELL. It isn't overexposed.

16 MRS HENNESSY. It isn't upside down.

17 HENNESSY. Out of focus.

1 BRIGGS. Boats. On the last one, no boats. On this one . . .
   [*indicating distant specks*] . . . boats.

2 CARTER. Perhaps you'd explain the significance of the boats,
   Mr Briggs.

   CARTER *turns to face the audience as* BRIGGS *launches into his
   explanation.*

3 BRIGGS. We decided to have a row on the lake. Twenty-five
   pence an hour, maximum four people to a boat. A little
   awkward with fifteen people. At any rate, I was negotia-
   ting with the man and then turned round to see the
   boats leaving the shore, with seven of our young friends
   in each . . .

4 MRS HENNESSY. Typical.

5 HENNESSY. Spoonfed.

6 MITCHELL. Very impetuous, our Linda.

7 BRIGGS. It was rather amusing, really. We'd pooled our
   spending money with myself in charge, and I said to the
   man . . . I'm in charge of the pool and you're in charge
   of the lake . . . but he didn't laugh. Next slide please.

   CARTER *pushes the slide through mechanically.*

   Same except the boats have moved. Next please.

   CARTER *changes the slide.*

   Same except I've moved. Next please.

   CARTER *changes the slide.*

   Same except we've both moved, it seemed I was in the
   way of the man's boat-hook.

   A spot on CARTER *as he turns to the audience.*

8 CARTER [*to audience*]. That's our Mr Briggs. Everybody else in
   the lifeboat and him waving from the shore, pausing
   only to focus on the Hereafter, a 50th at F 11, like a good
   Christian. I suppose if he was a good enough Christian
   he could have walked across to join them. But that's

to betray an attitude and we're not concerned with what, only with why.

2 BRIGGS. Next slide please.

CARTER *changes the slide : the next one is of the Youth Club dressed for swimming, with bikinis prominent, or strictly speaking, not prominent.*

[*conscious of audience unease*] I did wonder about this one . . .

3 AMY. It's when we went swimming.

4 MRS HENNESSY. Apparently.

5 MITCHELL. Overexposed?

6 BRIGGS. Shouldn't be. A 50th at F 11.

7 HENNESSY [*to Mitchell*]. Isn't that your Linda?

8 MITCHELL. Aye, that's her.

9 HENNESSY. She's a . . . fine big girl.

10 MITCHELL. Lot of people say that, yes . . .

11 MRS HENNESSY. They do, yes . . .

12 AMY [*factual amd honest*]. She's got a lovely figure.

13 BRIGGS. I didn't, in point of fact, go swimming myself. More of a non-participating lifeguard.

CARTER *turns quickly to the audience as* BRIGGS *continues silently in the background.*

14 CARTER. A non-participating lifeguard. Frightening thought, our Mr Briggs surrounded by all that youthful, virginal flesh. As far as can be ascertained with our limited facilities for research. Next slide please?

He anticipates BRIGGS's *request. The next slide is of a group of long-haired young people, indeterminate sex.*

15 BRIGGS. I wonder if you can guess what these are.

16 MITCHELL. Look like beatniks to me.

17 MRS HENNESSY. Stones.

18 HENNESSY. Spoonfed.

1 MITCHELL. Or rockers.

2 HENNESSY. Dropouts is it?

3 MRS HENNESSY. Teddy boys you mean.

4 CARTER. Fact-finding mission from the Arts Council?

5 BRIGGS. Beatniks I decided.

6 MRS HENNESSY. Spoonfed.

7 HENNESSY. Too much, too soon.

8 BRIGGS. They were camping in a field near the Youth Hostel·

9 MRS HENNESSY. I know what I'd do with them.

10 CARTER. What did you do with them, Mr Briggs?

11 BRIGGS. Well I must confess my first inclination was to pass by on the other side. But one evening, as I was on my way to see some rather interesting eggs in a nest by the riverbank, I paused by the tent and we had a free and frank exchange of views. I invited them to come to church with us the following day.

12 HENNESSY. And did they?

13 BRIGGS. Er . . . no.

14 MRS HENNESSY. Mollycoddled.

15 BRIGGS. But we parted on friendly terms, sharing a joke in fact.

16 CARTER. May we hear the joke, Mr Briggs.

17 BRIGGS. Certainly, it's quite clean . . . [*An uneasy laugh because to say things like that is, in itself, a little dirty.*] As I was talking to them, I could not but notice they were smoking some rather strange-smelling cigarettes. I simply said to them, if God had intended you to smoke, he would have provided chimneys in your heads.

    Pause.

18 CARTER. And did they laugh?

19 BRIGGS. Very loudly.

    CARTER *turns to the audience as* BRIGGS *continues silently.*

99

1 CARTER. If God had intended our Mr Briggs to give illustrated lectures he'd have welded a lectern to his chest and provided a thirteen amp power point up his nose.

2 BRIGGS. Next slide please.

CARTER changes the slide. The next is of a Brownie Pack on the march.

[*not looking at the screen*] This fine old parish church . . .

3 MITCHELL. Fine old Brownie Pack.

4 BRIGGS. Oh.

5 CARTER. Betrayed by Boots the Chemist's again.

6 MITCHELL. Your May Day carnival.

7 MRS HENNESSY. St Alban's Brownie Pack.

8 HENNESSY. St Bartholomew in the Market Place.

9 BRIGGS. Actually it's Great Gutter Lane Presbyterians.

10 MRS HENNESSY. Is it?

11 BRIGGS. Yes. Brown Owl used to work in our office until . . . until she left.

AMY smiles unseen, the only one to read between the lines apart from a deadpan CARTER.

Next slide please.

12 CARTER. That was the last one.

13 BRIGGS. Isn't there one of the parish church?

14 CARTER. Sorry.

15 BRIGGS. It's a fascinating little church, I made a few notes about its history from the very excellent official guide book . . .

16 CARTER. I'm sure we'd like to hear about its history, Mr Briggs . . .

17 HENNESSY. Just carry on, squire.

18 BRIGGS. Well I'd like you to imagine that these Brownies are a little stone church on the site of an old Roman encampment. Mediaeval monks, fleeing from persecution . . .

He continues in silence as CARTER *turns to the audience.*

1 CARTER. Mind you, you should have been here last week. Miss Veronica Bannister, J.P. Snippets from a magistrate's diary. A unique combination of boredom, sadism and flatulence. [*He looks at his watch.*] Never mind, soon be time for me hot cocoa and Late Night Line-up.

Broken by applause from the audience as BRIGGS *sits down.* CARTER *moves without a break into his speech of thanks.*

Thank you, Mr Briggs, for that refreshing and amusing discourse. It's good to know our young people are in such good hands.

2 MITCHELL. Here here. [*There is the merest hint of scepticism in* MITCHELL'*s tone.*]

3 CARTER. Two notices. There will be a committee meeting next Monday evening and the next meeting of the Friday Fellowship will be next Wednesday. This will be a joint affair called . . . We Do It Ourselves . . . with contributions from several members about things they do, as it were, themselves. Mrs Hennessy will speak on flower arranging and homemade jam . . .

4 MRS HENNESSY. I hope to squeeze in lemon curd, too.

5 CARTER. Good luck, Mrs Hennessy. Mr Mitchell will talk about servicing a mini-van without tears . . .

6 MITCHELL. Nearly always without tears.

Laughter.

7 CARTER. And Miss Amy Heslop will talk about recent trends in pop music.

8 MRS HENNESSY. Really?

9 CARTER. Much of it is full of sweetness and light, as indeed is Miss Amy Heslop . . . and now if you would all rise . . .

They stand, in attitudes of prayer.

We thank Thee for blessing this, our Fellowship, with Thy presence. May the spirit of this meeting be present at all times through all the earth. May Thy Dominion flourish and prosper. The Lord bless thee and keep thee, for Jesus Christ's sake . . .

2   ALL. Amen.

A pause, then the group breaks up.

3   BRIGGS. If you're a bit pushed next week, I can always give you ten minutes on photography.

4   CARTER. Into the darkroom, see what develops, thank you, Mr Briggs . . .

5   AMY. I'm not sure I'll be able to do my bit, what with G.C.E. and everything . . .

6   CARTER. The Lord will stand aside for G.C.E., I'm sure, Amy . . .

7   AMY. But I did promise and . . .

8   CARTER. I'll play my banjo if there are any awkward silences . . .

9   MITCHELL. Do you play the banjo, Mr Carter?

10 CARTER. We can but try.

11 MRS HENNESSY. The Reverend Bradley played the violin beautifully.

12 HENNESSY. Anything. Chopin, Beethoven . . . Chopin . . . you name it.

13 MRS HENNESSY. Just a word about the flowers.

14 CARTER. The flowers?

15 MRS HENNESSY. Did you have a word with Mrs Millican?

16 CARTER. I don't think I've had a word with Mrs Millican . . .

17 MRS HENNESSY. Perhaps you could.

18 CARTER. About . . . the flowers.

19 MRS HENNESSY. If you would have a word.

20 CARTER. I'll have a word. [*He has no idea what she's talking about.*]

21 HENNESSY. Can we give you a lift, Mr Briggs?

22 BRIGGS. No thanks, I promised myself the walk.

1 HENNESSY. You want to get yourself a dog.

2 BRIGGS. What I say is why spend good money on a dog when I can walk myself.

3 MITCHELL. They're good company.

4 AMY. I've got an elephant.

   Pause. The atmosphere, which has been restless and rootless, with CARTER *waiting for everybody to go home, finds a focus again.*

5 CARTER. How . . . er long have you had it?

6 AMY. It's a present. [*She presents* CARTER *with a small, homemade toy elephant.*] For your baby.

7 CARTER. That's very kind. What a jolly jumbo, hasn't he got a funny way of eating buns? Thank you, love.

8 MRS HENNESSY. Your wife not able to be with us this evening, Mr Carter?

9 CARTER. She was feeling a bit Wembley . . . sudden attack of the vapours . . .

10 MRS HENNESSY. I hope she's better soon.

11 CARTER. And what about your wife, Mr Mitchell?

12 MITCHELL. It's moved to her legs, thank you. Mind you, it's a blessing having the mini-van.

13 CARTER. It must be. Well . . .

   Pause.

14 HENNESSY. Well.

15 MITCHELL. Well.

16 BRIGGS. Well.

17 AMY. Well.

18 MRS HENNESSY. Well.

19 MITCHELL. Well if I can give anybody a lift, that's if it starts . . .

20 MRS HENNESSY. Amy's coming with us, aren't you, dear?

21 AMY. Yes please.

22 BRIGGS. And I'll have to push, I'd like to catch the fish shop while there's still halibut . . .

1   CARTER. The sweet life, Mr Briggs . . .

They filter out into the hallway, BRIGGS *lagging behind.* CARTER *looks at him.*

2   CARTER. Was there . . . something else?

3   BRIGGS. Yes . . . that is . . . no.

BRIGGS goes out, almost colliding with MITCHELL *as he comes in.*

4   CARTER. Was there . . . something else?

5   MITCHELL. Yes . . . that is . . . no.

MITCHELL goes out. CARTER *turns to audience.*

6   CARTER. Let me have men about me that are fat, that is, thin.

He goes out and we hear a chorus of goodnights, then the door closing. CARTER *comes in again. He picks up the elephant.*

7   CARTER. So I saw this little lad crying his eyes out. 'What's the matter?' I said. 'My elephant's dead,' he said. 'Your Daddy'll buy you another one,' I said. 'That's not what I'm crying about,' he said, 'I don't know how to bury the bugger.'

CARTER *goes out into the hallway. We hear him shout.*

[*off*] All right, you can come out now.

CARTER *comes into the room again. A pause then* MRS CARTER *comes in, in the best of health and spirits.*

8   MRS CARTER. Have all the Christians gone?

9   CARTER. Cortinas and mini-vans and feet are carrying them to the far-flung corners of the parish.

10 MRS CARTER. Are they all better people for this evening's fellowship in the sight of shhh you know who?

11 CARTER. There was a certain something in the air.

12 MRS CARTER. Airwick.

13 CARTER. I thought I could smell deodorant. No, what it was, was suspicion. Where's the vicar's wife? It seems the Reverend Mrs Bradley was always around. Great

worker, always making raffia mats and marmalade. Silver Shred tried to take her over.

2 MRS CARTER [*seeing the elephant*]. What's that?

3 CARTER. It's an elephant.

4 MRS CARTER. I thought so.

The doorbell rings.

The door.

5 CARTER. I thought so. Immediately I thought . . .

6 MRS CARTER. Billy Smart.

CARTER *gets up, goes to answer the door. Murmurs in the hall, then he comes in with* MITCHELL.

7 MITCHELL [*seeing* MRS CARTER]. Oh, I . . .

8 MRS CARTER. It's all right, we're not doing anything unseemly.

9 CARTER. My wife . . . Mr Mitchell . . .

10 MITCHELL. Pleased to meet you at last, Mrs Carter.

11 MRS CARTER. Have you got a shop?

12 MITCHELL. No.

13 CARTER. Mr Hennessy's got a shop.

14 MRS CARTER. In that case your wife's ill.

15 MITCHELL. That's right.

16 MRS CARTER. How is she?

17 MITCHELL. It's moved to her legs. And how are your . . . vapours?

18 MRS CARTER. Coming along nicely, thank you. [*Sudden thought* . You've got a mini-van.

19 MITCHELL. That's right.

20 CARTER. I hope it hasn't broken down.

21 MITCHELL. Oh no. I'm concerned about the battery, it's no good pretending otherwise but . . . mechanically it's very sound. No, it's not the mini-van.

Pause.

1 CARTER. Something else?

2 MITCHELL. Yes . . . that is . . . yes. [*He looks across at* MRS CARTER.] Something . . . delicate.

3 CARTER. My hot cocoa.

4 MRS CARTER. If you'll excuse me, Mr Mitchell . . . I have to see a man about some hot cocoa. [*She goes out.*]

5 MITCHELL. I drove round the block a couple of times, give the others chance to get away.

6 CARTER. I see. [*He doesn't.*]

7 MITCHELL. I thought it might be best, I mean, with the best will in the world, people see things and they talk.

8 CARTER. They're only human.

9 MITCHELL. You've put your finger on it. Human.

10 CARTER. Human?

11 MITCHELL. I didn't choose the word lightly.

12 CARTER. Has something . . . human been going on?

13 MITCHELL. Did go on . . . in the past tense.

14 CARTER. That's a blessing, anyway, if it's over and done with.

15 MITCHELL. Over but not done with, I fancy.

Pause.

16 CARTER. Who?

17 MITCHELL. Mr Briggs.

18 CARTER. Mr Briggs?

19 MITCHELL. The Youth Club Easter outing.

20 CARTER. What about it?

21 MITCHELL. I have reason to believe that a certain incident took place.

Pause.

22 CARTER. What sort of incident?

23 MITCHELL. A certain incident. An unfortunate incident.

24 CARTER. I don't really know what you're talking about, Mr Mitchell.

1 MITCHELL. An incident which I can only describe as physical.

2 CARTER [*trying to work it out*]. An unfortunate physical incident . . .

3 MITCHELL. Very unfortunate, yes.

4 CARTER. What has it to do with Mr Briggs?

5 MITCHELL. He took part in it.

6 CARTER. Mr Briggs?

7 MITCHELL. Yes. The man we entrust, year by year, with the flower of our youth, with the slowly budding seeds of our . . . yes, Mr Briggs.

8 CARTER. And who else?

9 MITCHELL. He was in sole charge.

10 CARTER. No, I mean who else was involved in this unfortunate physical incident?

11 MITCHELL. Linda.

12 CARTER. Linda who?

13 MITCHELL. My daughter.

14 CARTER. I'm not quite clear what you're accusing Mr Briggs of doing.

15 MITCHELL. Molesting my daughter.

  Pause.

16 CARTER. To what extent?

17 MITCHELL. It's difficult to be precise about molesting.

18 CARTER. Are you telling me they had sexual intercourse?

19 MITCHELL [*stunned*]. I'm astonished.

20 CARTER. I beg your pardon?

21 MITCHELL. I never thought to hear such language, not from a man of the cloth . . .

22 CARTER. I'm simply trying to find out what you want to tell me . . .

23 MITCHELL. But to suggest that our Linda . . .

24 CARTER. All right, all right . . . but you'll have to spell it out, Mr Mitchell, however painful . . .

1   MITCHELL. It's difficult, when it's your own flesh and . . . your own daughter.

2   CARTER. You'll have to try.

Pause.

3   MITCHELL. I have every reason to believe that Mr Briggs touched my daughter.

4   CARTER. Touched her?

5   MITCHELL. Touched her.

6   CARTER. Where?

7   MITCHELL. On the banks of Lake Windermere.

8   CARTER. Whereabouts on your daughter?

9   MITCHELL. I have reason to believe that Mr Briggs touched my daughter on the upper part of her body.

10 CARTER. Is that all?

11 MITCHELL. Isn't it enough?

12 CARTER. All I mean is, it's not a major disaster.

13 MITCHELL. Not a fit subject for joking.

14 CARTER. I'm not joking.

15 MITCHELL. Some people think you make too many jokes.

16 CARTER. The thing is, if Mr Briggs merely touched the girl, as you describe, at least she isn't going to have a baby, anything like that.

17 MITCHELL. So because Linda isn't having a baby, Briggs must not be brought to justice and punished, is that what you mean?

18 CARTER. It's a minor transgression, not a major crime. And I haven't heard any evidence yet.

19 MITCHELL. My word should be enough, shouldn't it?

20 CARTER. How did you find out?

21 MITCHELL. She told me.

22 CARTER. But it happened two months ago, assuming the alleged physical incident took place . . .

1   MITCHELL. She's obviously been worried about it, afraid to talk.

2   CARTER. Why did she talk after all this time?

3   MITCHELL. I told her Mr Briggs was giving an illustrated lecture about the Easter holiday. She said, I bet he doesn't tell you everything. [*Pause.*] And two days previous, I told her how Mr Hennessy had said, after Church on Sunday, what a fine big girl she was growing into and she said, Briggsy thinks so as well, she said. So I challenged her. Or at least, her mother did.

4   CARTER. And she told her mother that he'd touched her, unquote, and Mrs Mitchell told you to tell me.

5   MITCHELL. More or less.

6   CARTER. Has Linda been emotionally disturbed by the incident?

7   MITCHELL. What?

8   CARTER. Upset? Since Easter? Has it affected her?

9   MITCHELL. No. Nothing affects her. Always off dancing and that.

10 CARTER. So it's a rather silly little incident that's best forgotten . . .

11 MITCHELL. You can't forget things like that. Not when it's immoral.

12 CARTER. Can't you? I forget things all the time.

13 MITCHELL. You haven't done anything like that.

14 CARTER. I've had my momentary fumbles. Nothing to boast about but . . .

15 MITCHELL. This man occupies a position of trust, we entrust him with . . .

16 CARTER. The flower of our youth, and once in about a hundred and fifty years he does something a little stupid and thoughtless. And no doubt apologized immediately. What do you want me to do?

17 MITCHELL. I want it all cleared up in a proper manner.

1 CARTER. Your wife wants it all cleared up.

2 MITCHELL. We both want it clearing up.

3 CARTER. Yes. I can see you do. [*Pause.*] Did Briggs leap on Linda in a mad passion?

4 MITCHELL. This is a new side of you, Mr Carter . . .

5 CARTER. Did he? I still don't know what I'm clearing up.

6 MITCHELL. It seems . . . I gather . . . apparently, Linda tells me, he was more like . . . shy with it.

7 CARTER. All I can do is talk to the people concerned, your daughter and Mr Briggs, and give whatever guidance I'm able to . . . but only at their request.

8 MITCHELL. Is that all?

9 CARTER. What did you want? A public execution?

10 MITCHELL. It just seems a pity that's all.

11 CARTER. Why?

12 MITCHELL. You wouldn't consider . . . just contemplate telling the police. . . ?

13 CARTER. No.

14 MITCHELL. This man, occupying as he does a position of trust . . .

15 CARTER. No.

16 MITCHELL. Endowed with the flower of our youth.

17 CARTER. No.

18 MITCHELL. Intimate physical incidents of this kind are an offence in law. [*Pause.*] But you wouldn't tell the police?

19 CARTER. No.

20 MITCHELL. That *is* a pity.

21 CARTER. Why is it a pity?

22 MITCHELL. Because I've already told them myself.

23 CARTER. You went to the police station?

24 MITCHELL. I've always found it the best place when seeking policemen. Took our Linda, she made a statement.

25 CARTER. Did she go voluntarily? Or because you forced her?

1 MITCHELL. I showed her that it was her responsibility to society at large.

2 CARTER. You must be very proud.

3 MITCHELL. I mean where does it stop? What would happen if everybody did it? Anyhow, it looks as if they'll charge him. They know the difference between right and wrong even if you don't.

4 CARTER. No, no, it's an achievement, getting your daughter in the News of the World, at seventeen. Takes some people years.

5 MITCHELL. I don't think there's any more to be said. My wife will be expecting me and . . .

6 CARTER. Your battery's giving trouble.

7 MITCHELL. It is, to be honest. [*He crosses to the door.*] Were you serious about the News of the World?

8 CARTER. Unless the editor hears your prayers.

   MITCHELL *nods.*

9 MITCHELL. I'll .. er . . . see you on Sunday. [*He goes out.*]

   MRS CARTER *comes in.*

10 MRS CARTER. And the moral is, keep your filthy hands to yourself.

11 CARTER. Did you listen?

12 MRS CARTER. I was listening at the serving hatch.

13 CARTER. Open planning, it's changed the whole nature of espionage.

14 MRS CARTER. What'll happen?

15 CARTER. Justice will rear its ugly head, I expect.

   The lighting changes.

16 MRS CARTER. You've missed Late Night Line-up.

17 CARTER [*as a policeman*]. Edward Sebastian Briggs I'd like you to assist us in our inquiries into a nasty little spot of bother down by the lake . . . if you'd just stand in this line . . .

CARTER, *as* BRIGGS, *stands in an imaginary identity parade.* MRS CARTER *walks along the line, reacting to each imaginary individual in turn.*

1   MRS CARTER. No. He wasn't a negro . . . [*On to the next.*] No, he didn't have a wooden leg . . . [*On to the next.*] No, he wasn't a dwarf . . . [*On to the next.*] No, he didn't have a red beard and the Order of the Garter . . . [*On to the next.*] No, he didn't play the harp . . . [*On to* CARTER.] That's him, that's the filthy swine. [*Very flat and undramatic.*] That's the man what dented my virtue, that is the father of my trauma, he should be thrashed within an inch of his wife.

2   CARTER. Briggs is a bachelor.

3   MRS CARTER. Sorry.

4   CARTER [*as policeman*]. Edward Briggs, too long bachelor of this parish, I arrest you in the name of the Law, the Queen, the Confederation of British Industry and members of the B.B.C. Drama Repertory Company. You are charged with vulgar assault on sweet Linda Mitchell, spinster of this parish . . . [*reverting to own voice*] but not for long according to young Lennie Tanner . . .

5   MRS CARTER. Really?

6   CARTER. Yes. And often.

7   MRS CARTER [*as policeman, to* CARTER *as* BRIGGS]. Anything you say may be taken down and used in evidence against you. Anything you took down may be used in evidence against you.

8   CARTER. Anything Linda Mitchell took down . . .?

9   MRS CARTER. Ask Lennie Tanner.

10 CARTER. Pity about missing Late Night Line-up.

11 MRS CARTER. Edward Briggs, how do you plead?

12 CARTER. If you prick me, do I not plead?

13 MRS CARTER. I said bleedin' plead, not bleedin' bleed.

14 CARTER. Guilty's cheapest, legal charges being what they are. Guilty, my lord, lady. Lady?

1   MRS CARTER. Edward Briggs. Before I pass sentence, is there
    anything you wish to say on your behalf, any honest
    citizen who will produce testimonials?

2   CARTER. The Reverend James Carter, Vicar of St Amber's.

3   MRS CARTER. Sensation in court. Vicar speaks. Sex maniac
    reveals secret friends among clergy. Read all about it.

    And now CARTER *is speaking in court on behalf of* BRIGGS. *We
    should understand that this is the real thing.*

4   CARTER. I know Edward Briggs as a loyal member of my
    church and a devoted worker in the parish. He is chair-
    man of the church committee and has been Youth Club
    leader for the last seventeen years. In my experience Mr
    Briggs is loyal, trustworthy and dedicated to those things
    he holds most important in life, his work and his faith.
    I ask the Court to share my faith, hope and under-
    standing.

    The lights revert to normal.

5   MRS CARTER. What else did you say to the magistrate?

6   CARTER. Blessed are the merciful, I reminded him.

7   MRS CARTER. Promises, promises . . . so what happened?

8   CARTER. Briggs pleaded guilty and they gave him a condi-
    tional discharge.

9   MRS CARTER. What's that?

10 CARTER. It means they won't hang him this time but if he
    does it again, they'll hang him twice.

11 MRS CARTER. The accused left the court without a stain on his
    trousers. But the worst is yet to come.

12 CARTER. What worst?

13 MRS CARTER. When his fellow-Christians get hold of him.

    CARTER *nods.*

14 CARTER. Committee meeting tonight. We'll see.

15 MRS CARTER. It'll be cross your legs I've only got one nail,
    Mr Briggs, you'll see.

1 CARTER. If he turns up. [*Pause.*] Are you going to bless the meeting with your presence?

2 MRS CARTER. For three or four minutes. I've got my own committee meeting at the Four in Hand.

3 CARTER. The committee of seven?

4 MRS CARTER. Small town. Can't manage a hundred.

5 CARTER. Harry Bainbridge, chairman?

6 MRS CARTER. Mao Tse Bainbridge, the one and only.

7 CARTER. And Hairy Dan, the ethnic folk singer from the College of Technology?

8 MRS CARTER. All the old favourites, yes.

9 CARTER. What are you planning as the next blow for freedom?

10 MRS CARTER. We're marching on J. Snelgrove and Sons, Manufacturing Joiners. . .

11 CARTER. Any special reason?

12 MRS CARTER. They make flagpoles.

13 CARTER. Somebody's got to make flagpoles, otherwise the flags would just fall limp to the ground.

14 MRS CARTER. Nobody disputes that.

15 CARTER. Mind you, what would happen if everybody made flagpoles, be anti-social, dangerous too . . . [*He stumbles about the stage, running into imaginary flagpoles in all directions.*]

16 MRS CARTER. They're making flagpoles for segregated sports stadiums in South Africa.

17 CARTER. That's worth marching a few hundred yards, yes . . .

MRS CARTER *is digging deep into a cupboard.*

What are you doing?

18 MRS CARTER. Looking for a banner in the files.

19 CARTER. Bet you a tanner in the Oxfam box there's nothing about flagpoles.

She unfurls a banner: *ALDERMASTON 1961.*

Is it really all those years ago?

1 MRS CARTER [*raising the banner high*]. Ah, we were so young . . .

2 CARTER. And she looked so pale and I said, excuse me, my child that pole must be hurting you where it's sticking into your . . .

3 MRS CARTER. Abdomen.

4 CARTER. Approximately.

5 MRS CARTER. And I thought, oh lawks, I'm being chatted up by a bishop.

6 CARTER. And I thought you were an actress.

7 MRS CARTER. So we shared the load together, all the way to the Haymarket where we were attacked by long-haired deviationists from the Harlequins Rugby Club.

8 CARTER [*to audience*]. Or so we like to think.

9 MRS CARTER [*to him, with real affection*]. I never regretted it, neither.

10 CARTER. Nor me neither.

> *They kiss, not sloppy.* CARTER *breaks off, picks up another banner: a picture of* MACMILLAN *with caption* MAC, YOU NEVER HAD IT.

11 MRS CARTER. Got rid of him, anyway.

12 CARTER. Still got the bomb. Means we're drawing one all.

> *She unfurls another:* ANTI APARTHEID.

13 MRS CARTER. Losing two one.

> *He unfurls another:* PEACE IN VIETNAM.

14 CARTER. Losing three one.

> *She unfurls another:* MAKE LOVE NOT WAR.

That about squares it. Call it a draw.

15 MRS CARTER. What about this?

> *She unfurls another:* SHEFFIELD WEDNESDAY FOR THE CUP.

16 CARTER. Never did understand that one.

1   MRS CARTER. Don't even know if they won.

2   CARTER. Keep it as a swop.

3   MRS CARTER. Nothing about flagpoles. We'll have to make a
new one.

4   CARTER. We?

5   MRS CARTER. Yes. You're coming on the march.

6   CARTER. Supposing my conscience dictates otherwise? Perhaps I think the sight of a well-made British flagpole will
stimulate liberal thoughts among white South African
sprinters and long jumpers.

7   MRS CARTER. We took a vote at our last meeting. Four votes
to three in favour of having God on our side.

8   CARTER. You've got four believers on the committee? What
sort of committee's that?

9   MRS CARTER. Three militant atheists and four don't cares,
but they like you. Anyway everybody wants you to
come, the vote was whether you should wear your
collar or not.

10 CARTER. If I come in a poloneck sweater God isn't on our
side, is that it?

11 MRS CARTER. I'd be happier that way. Insofar as I'd rather have
you than God, something's better than nothing even
if it's only you.

12 CARTER. Flatterer.

13 MRS CARTER. But the will of the majority says Jesus gear.

14 CARTER [*hands together*]. I'll speak to Head Office.

The doorbell rings.

15 MRS CARTER. That's your lot isn't it?

16 CARTER [*hands still clasped*]. I thought for a minute it might be
a sign.

17 MRS CARTER. Rehearsal, quick.

MRS CARTER *has a piece of paper, with notes written on. As* CARTER
runs through the details, she checks her answers on this—her crib.

1 CARTER. Hennessy.

2 MRS CARTER. Shopkeeper. Reactionary. Good for trade discounts, nothing else.

3 CARTER. Mrs Hennessy.

4 MRS CARTER. Social climber, don't mention flowers.

5 CARTER. Mitchell.

6 MRS CARTER. Mini-van and a wife with bad legs.

7 CARTER. Amy.

8 MRS CARTER. Wonderful Amy, youth club, O levels . . .

9 CARTER. A levels.

10 MRS CARTER. A levels.

11 CARTER. Briggs.

12 MRS CARTER. Dirty beast. Misunderstood dirty beast.

Doorbell rings again.

13 CARTER. Be nice. [*He goes to answer the door.*]

14 MRS CARTER [*to audience*]. Yea though I walk through the valley of the shadow of death I will fear no evil for these boots were made for walking and one of these days will walk all over Thee. Thou.

CARTER *comes in with* AMY.

15 CARTER. Amy. My wife.

16 MRS CARTER. Hello Amy.

17 AMY. Hello Mrs Carter.

MRS CARTER *checks her piece of paper.*

18 MRS CARTER. Find yourself the most comfortable seat.

AMY *dutifully picks the least comfortable seat.*

And thank you for the elephant.

19 AMY. Did your baby like it?

20 MRS CARTER. Delicious, he said. You made it yourself?

21 AMY. Yes.

1 MRS CARTER. I can't make anything.

2 AMY. The Reverend Bradley's wife used to . . .

3 MRS CARTER. Marmalade?

4 AMY. Yes. [*Pause.*] Is that why you don't come to church?

5 MRS CARTER. Because I'm trying to make marmalade?

6 AMY. Because of the baby?

7 MRS CARTER. Partly.

8 AMY. I could babysit if you like. I could go to morning service.

9 MRS CARTER. There are other complications. [*Pause.*] How are the O levels?

10 AMY. A levels.

11 MRS CARTER. Damn. A levels.

The doorbell rings.

12 CARTER. No dear, let me go. [*As he is halfway to the door.*]

13 AMY [*quietly*]. Do you think Mr Briggs will come tonight?

14 MRS CARTER. I don't see why not, do you?

15 AMY. No.

CARTER *comes in with* MITCHELL.

16 MRS CARTER. Good evening Mr Mitchell, find yourself the most comfortable seat.

17 MITCHELL. Thank you Mrs Carter. [*He sits down in the least comfortable seat available.*]

18 MRS CARTER. How is your mini-van?

19 MITCHELL. Got a funny knock at the rear end.

20 MRS CARTER. And Mrs Mitchell?

21 MITCHELL. It's centralizing on her knees. Very odd. [*Uneasy pause. To* CARTER] Do you think . . . a certain party will show his face?

22 CARTER. He knows about the meeting.

23 MITCHELL. You'll appreciate my position. [*Uneasy pause. To* AMY] How are the O levels?

1 AMY. A levels.

2 MITCHELL. A levels.

MRS CARTER *laughs as the doorbell rings.*

3 CARTER. I'll go. [*He goes to the door.*]

4 MITCHELL. Been very cold.

5 MRS CARTER. Yes.

CARTER *comes in with* MR *and* MRS HENNESSY.

6 CARTER. My wife.

7 MRS CARTER. Mr and Mrs Hennessy, how nice.

8 HENNESSY. How do you do.

9 MRS HENNESSY. Delighted to meet you after all this time.

10 MRS CARTER. And how's the retail grocery trade?

11 HENNESSY. Well it's never as good as you'd like it to be.

12 MRS CARTER. Eight per cent unemployment doesn't help.

13 MRS HENNESSY. They never set anything by when times are good. Just spend, spend, spend.

14 HENNESSY. Then they look you in the eye and ask for tick.

15 MRS CARTER. Must be very difficult for you . . . oh, please take the most comfortable seats that are left . . .

Just as the HENNESSYS *are about to sit in the two remaining seats, easily the most comfortable that are in the room and clearly their ancient right.*

16 HENNESSY. Is . . . a certain party coming?

17 CARTER. We don't know.

18 MITCHELL. He's leaving it late if he is.

19 HENNESSY. I think you should take the chair, Mr Carter, can't hold up the business of the parish because of one man's frailties.

20 MRS HENNESSY. How are the O levels, dear?

21 AMY. A levels.

22 MRS HENNESSY. Silly me.

MRS HENNESSY *looks for something in her bag as* AMY *replies though nobody listens.*

1 AMY. I'm happy about maths but biology's a bit of a problem.

2 CARTER. Funny, I always found biology pretty easy. Eyes on the ball, head down and follow through. [*He mimes a golf shot.*]

3 MRS HENNESSY. Have you spoken to Mrs Millican yet?

4 CARTER. Er, no, not yet.

5 MRS HENNESSY. About the flowers.

6 CARTER. The flowers, yes, I remember.

7 MRS HENNESSY. If you could have a word . . .

8 CARTER. I'll have a word, about the . . . flowers.

9 MITCHELL. Can we get started then? I'm a bit concerned about my parking light. Loose connection.

10 HENNESSY. Lot of them about.

11 MRS CARTER. Well if you'll excuse me . . . [*She gets up to go.*]

12 MRS HENNESSY. Are you leaving us already Mrs Carter?

13 CARTER. My wife has another meeting to attend, alas. Doing good works of course, I can vouch for that, good works.

14 MRS CARTER. It's the local branch of Pile the Pavement with Pennies for Poverty Week.

15 HENNESSY. I haven't heard about that.

16 MRS CARTER. Just laying plans. It'll soon be emblazoned across the bosom of the Nation.

17 MRS HENNESSY [*uncertainly*]. Good.

18 MRS CARTER. Goodnight everybody.

She goes out to a chorus of polite goodnights.

19 MRS HENNESSY. Pity your wife couldn't spend more time with us.

20 CARTER. Trouble is, if it isn't the vapours, it's piles . . . of pennies I mean.

21 MITCHELL. Perhaps you'd like to take the chair, Mr Carter, in view of our loose connections.

1   CARTER. Is there any particular chair?

2   HENNESSY. A certain party generally sits where you're sitting.

3   CARTER. So I'll stay right here and take the chair. [*Pause. Deep breath.*] I declare open this meeting of the St Amber's Church Committee and call upon the Honorary Secretary to read the minutes of the last meeting.

     Pause.

4   MRS HENNESSY. I think I've left them in my other bag.

5   HENNESSY. That's a good start.

6   MRS HENNESSY. You didn't remind me.

7   MITCHELL. We could take the minutes as read, Mr Chairman.

8   AMY. I propose we take the minutes as read.

9   MRS HENNESSY. They haven't been circulated.

10 HENNESSY. So nobody's read them.

11 CARTER. You're suggesting it's impossible to take them as read, if nobody has, as it were, read them?

12 HENNESSY. It's a clever trick but it's impossible.

13 CARTER. We have a proposal that they be taken as read.

14 MRS HENNESSY. Could I propose that my husband slips home for my other bag, it wouldn't take more than twenty minutes.

15 CARTER. We have to vote on Amy's proposal first.

16 MITCHELL. We were all at the meeting, we remember what happened.

17 CARTER. All those in favour? That the minutes be taken as read.

     AMY *and* MITCHELL *raise their hands.*

     Against?

     MR *and* MRS HENNESSY *raise their hands.*

     I'll cast my vote in favour. The minutes are taken as read.

18 HENNESSY. You should be writing this down, dear.

1 MRS HENNESSY. How can I? The minute book's in my other bag.

2 MITCHELL. I'll keep a few notes for you. You can sort it out after.

3 CARTER. Good.

4 MRS HENNESSY. I'd do the same but my pen's in my other . . .

5 CARTER. Are there any corrections to the minutes?

6 HENNESSY. Well, since they haven't been circulated and . . .

7 CARTER. We understand. [*Hesitates.*] Are there any matters arising from the minutes?

8 HENNESSY. Well, since they haven't been . . .

9 MRS HENNESSY. Oh, be quiet! [*Pause.*] Dear.

10 HENNESSY. It's just that we should clarify the situation.

11 MRS HENNESSY. I think there was something in the minutes about the flowers . . .

12 CARTER. I think we should defer that until I've had a word with Mrs Millican.

MRS HENNESSY *shrugs.*

So is it the wish that I sign these minutes as a true and accurate record of the last meeting?

A chorus of agreement.

13 MITCHELL. Except that you can't.

14 CARTER. With that reservation, yes . . .

15 MITCHELL. No objections from this quarter.

16 CARTER. The next item is the Treasurer's Report. Mr Mitchell, can we have your report?

17 MITCHELL. Well I don't in point of fact have the books with me, what with the wife's bit of bother and various loose connections but I can tell you there is no material change in the situation. Working from memory . . . income nil, expenditure nil, bank interest, since we have no money in the deposit account, nil. No change, in more ways than one.

Pause.

1 CARTER. Are there any questions arising from the Treasurer's Report?

No response.

May I have a proposal that we accept the Treasurer's Report?

2 HENNESSY. I propose we accept the Treasurer's Report.

3 AMY. Seconded.

A look from MRS HENNESSY, *who wanted to second it.* CARTER *looks round the others, draws the obvious conclusion.*

4 CARTER. Carried unanimously. The next item is a report from the Youth in Christ committee . . . Miss Heslop.

5 AMY. Well there isn't much what with everybody being busy with A levels . . . or O levels . . .

6 CARTER. We understand.

7 AMY. But we have arranged a lecture on the 27th . . .

8 MRS HENNESSY. Oh good, what have you arranged?

9 AMY. An illustrated talk on Easter in the Lake District by Mr Briggs.

10 CARTER. Should be very interesting.

11 MRS HENNESSY. Do you really think . . .?

12 CARTER [*breaking in*]. Is it the wish of the meeting that we accept Miss Heslop's report? Carried unanimously, good.

Looks from MRS HENNESSY, *aware* CARTER *has rushed it through.*

Next item, ladies committee. [*with great charm*] Mrs Hennessy? Can you tell us what the good ladies have been up to?

13 MRS HENNESSY. I have nothing to report whatsoever, in the absence of Mrs Millican.

14 CARTER [*looking around*]. Well there is no question about it . . . Mrs Millican is absent.

15 MRS HENNESSY. That concludes my report, Mr Chairman.

1   CARTER. May I have a proposal that we accept Mrs Hennessy's report?

2   HENNESSY. I propose we accept Mrs . . . er, my wife's report

    Pause.

3   MITCHELL. Sorry . . . seconded.

4   CARTER. And carried unanimously. We now come to . . . any other business. Is there any other business?

5   HENNESSY. There is something I'd like to raise.

6   CARTER. Please feel free, Mr Hennessy.

7   HENNESSY. I expect we will, in the fullness of time, be planning further social events of the kind we used to have in the Reverend Bradley's day . . .

8   CARTER. I'm sure.

9   HENNESSY. Just to say I've been talking things over with some of my business colleagues and they are happy to continue giving St Amber's a substantial discount on all foodstuffs and so on . . .

10 MRS HENNESSY. Boiled ham, scones, sausage rolls, individual trifles, we had some lovely spreads, didn't we?

11 MITCHELL. Oh yes, grand.

12 HENNESSY. At a considerable saving.

13 CARTER. I suggest we record our appreciation of Mr Hennessy's good work and ask him not to ring us, we will ring him.

    Murmured agreement, but a hint that HENNESSY *and his wife feel not quite sufficiently appreciated by* CARTER.

14 CARTER. Is there any other business?

    A long, long pause.

15 MRS HENNESSY. Yes, there is.

16 CARTER. Yes?

    Another long pause.

17 MRS HENNESSY. I don't think it's a woman's responsibility.

1   CARTER. Isn't it?

2   MRS HENNESSY. I don't think so, no.

    Another long pause.

3   CARTER. If there is no further business I declare ...

4   MRS HENNESSY [*breaking in*]. But there is! [*She turns on* HENNESSY.]
    Go on!

5   HENNESSY. I er ... well ... I think my wife means ... a certain
    party.

6   MRS HENNESSY. There. It took long enough for you to say it.

7   CARTER. He hasn't actually said anything, has he? Has he?
    [*He appeals to the others.*]

8   HENNESSY. I have spoken what lies in everybody's mind.

9   CARTER. But what about it?

10 HENNESSY. I feel it's not something we can easily discuss with
    er ... [*He looks at* AMY.]

11 CARTER. Miss Heslop is a committee member. If it's a com-
    mittee matter ...

12 HENNESSY. Now that's a good point. Is it a committee matter?

13 MRS HENNESSY. Of course it is!

14 HENNESSY. Of course it is.

15 MITCHELL. I'm happy to withdraw if ...

16 CARTER. Not unless your loose connection's playing up?

17 MITCHELL. Oh no, just ...

18 HENNESSY. Declaring an interest?

19 MITCHELL. So to speak.

20 AMY. Is it Mr Briggs you wanted to talk about?

    Pause.

21 HENNESSY. That sums it up, yes.

22 MRS HENNESSY. That's why we wondered about Amy.

23 CARTER. If we're talking about Mr Briggs and his relationship

to young people, it seems reasonable to have a young people with us.

2 MRS HENNESSY [*shrugs*]. Well you're not my daughter, Amy ...

3 AMY. I know.

Pause.

4 CARTER. So what about Mr Briggs.

5 HENNESSY. I think we should discuss his position.

6 CARTER. His position?

7 HENNESSY. Yes.

8 MRS HENNESSY. I think so too.

9 CARTER. Mr Mitchell?

10 MITCHELL. I think we should discuss his position.

11 CARTER. Well ... what about his position?

Pause.

12 HENNESSY. If you don't mind, I'd like to be absolutely frank about this.

13 MITCHELL. It's the only way.

14 HENNESSY. I think his position is delicate.

15 MRS HENNESSY. Very delicate.

16 MITCHELL. Yes.

17 CARTER. Let's be specific about it. When you heard about what had happened ... what were your reactions? Mr Hennessy?

18 HENNESSY. I said to myself ... and I said it to Mrs Hennessy ... we shall have to discuss Mr Briggs position ... seriously.

19 CARTER. Mrs Hennessy?

20 MRS HENNESSY. It made me sick.

21 CARTER. Really.

22 MRS HENNESSY. I couldn't find words.

23 CARTER. Mr Mitchell?

24 MITCHELL. I went to the police if you remember.

1 MRS HENNESSY. Quite right too.

2 MITCHELL. It wasn't in the News of the World by the way.

3 MRS HENNESSY [*quietly*]. No, I couldn't find it, either.

4 CARTER. Amy. What were your reactions?

5 HENNESSY. Is it fair to ask . . .?

6 CARTER. Yes.

7 AMY. I think it's all a bit sad.

8 HENNESSY. We know that.

9 AMY. I feel sorry for Mr Briggs.

10 MRS HENNESSY. Mr Briggs will have to be watched.

11 AMY. It depends on the circumstances.

12 HENNESSY. What circumstances?

13 AMY. I don't know. But it does.

14 MRS HENNESSY. I don't understand what you mean, dear.

15 AMY. We don't know exactly what happened.

16 MITCHELL. We know enough.

17 AMY. But there's some girls, I'm not saying Linda, but there's some girls, you know, that might be as much to blame as the man.

18 MITCHELL. Not Linda.

19 AMY. I'm not saying Linda.

20 MITCHELL. But Linda's who it was.

21 CARTER. I think what Amy means is do we blame any man for anything he does, whatever the circumstances?

22 MITCHELL. Of course we do, when it's anything that affects the flower of our youth.

23 HENNESSY. It's simple enough. Thou shalt not kill, thou shalt not steal, thou shalt not commit . . . adultery.

24 AMY. It wasn't adultery.

25 HENNESSY. It's the same sort of thing.

26 CARTER. What about stealing?

27 MRS HENNESSY. It wasn't stealing.

1 MITCHELL. You could say he stole a little of my daughter's innocence.

2 CARTER. We're all against stealing, I suppose?

3 MRS HENNESSY. Of course.

4 HENNESSY. I don't steal.

5 MRS HENNESSY. Neither do I.

6 MITCHELL. Never stolen anything myself.

7 HENNESSY. Thou shalt not steal, that's all there is to it.

8 AMY. I steal.

   Pause.

9 MITCHELL. You don't, do you?

10 AMY. Yes.

11 CARTER. What do you steal?

12 AMY. Exercise books. From school, I've got about a dozen at home. Use them for writing things in.

13 MITCHELL. That's not stealing.

14 HENNESSY. That's not what we mean.

15 MITCHELL. I mean I've had the odd bit of timber from work, but that's not stealing.

16 AMY. What is it?

17 MITCHELL. Well it's . . .

18 MRS HENNESSY. Not stealing . . .

19 HENNESSY. No.

20 CARTER. Taking something that doesn't strictly belong to you . . .

21 MITCHELL. It's more like helping yourself.

22 CARTER. Well what about Mr Hennessy?

23 HENNESSY. Nothing to do with me, nobody helps themselves from my shop. Anybody tries it, we prosecute, you've got to be firm with them.

24 CARTER. I wasn't thinking of that. Supposing you've got some item in your shop and if you sell it at six pence you make a reasonable profit . . .

1 HENNESSY. Yes.

2 CARTER. Supposing you find you can sell this item at nine pence and people will still pay . . .

3 HENNESSY. Just the sort of thing I'm looking for.

4 MRS HENNESSY. I should say so, yes.

5 CARTER. Aren't you stealing the extra three pence?

6 HENNESSY. Certainly not.

7 AMY. You are a bit . . .

8 HENNESSY. It's normal business practice.

9 MRS HENNESSY. If people are gullible then . . .

10 CARTER. Then you have the right to take them for a ride?

11 HENNESSY. It's a competitive world, when you're in business, you do as the Romans do, that's life.

12 CARTER. So we all steal in our various ways.

13 HENNESSY. Not stealing. Normal business practice.

14 CARTER. A bit of timber from work . . .

15 MITCHELL. Helping yourself, borrowing more like.

16 CARTER. Borrowing but not returning. Adding three pence to the retail price of an article.

17 MRS HENNESSY. And getting things through the trade to benefit the church, don't let us forget that.

18 HENNESSY. I'm not a man to quibble about a bit of discount.

19 CARTER. Exercise books from school.

20 AMY. Yes, that's stealing.

21 MRS HENNESSY. It's unfair to pick on the youngest.

22 HENNESSY. It all depends on the circumstances.

23 MRS HENNESSY. Life is like that.

24 MITCHELL. We didn't make life the way it is.

25 AMY. It's still wrong.

26 MRS HENNESSY. You're a little young, Amy, to be telling us how to live our lives.

27 CARTER. Nobody is telling anybody, we each have our own individual choice to make.

1 HENNESSY. All I can say is, I'm sorry you feel this way about the retail grocery trade.

Pause.

2 CARTER. What way?

3 HENNESSY. Well you've got to admit, you have rather had a go at us, haven't you?

4 CARTER. If you've got nothing to hide there's no problem.

5 MRS HENNESSY. I think what my husband means is, that this is the sort of discussion we're not accustomed to on this committee.

6 AMY. It's usually more flowers and bazaars.

7 CARTER. It's religion we're talking about Mrs Hennessy.

8 MRS HENNESSY. I don't ever remember the Reverend Bradley discussing religion with us, do you, dear?

9 HENNESSY. Hardly ever.

10 MITCHELL. Well doesn't it all depend on the circumstances?

11 HENNESSY. My feeling exactly. It's all circumstances.

12 MRS HENNESSY. You've got to consider the circumstances.

13 CARTER. We all agree. We must consider the circumstances.

14 AMY. That's what I said at the start.

15 CARTER. And now they all agree with you Amy. We don't condemn a man for what he's done without looking at the circumstances first. We don't condemn Mr Briggs because . . .

16 MRS HENNESSY. We do. Any man that does what he did should be condemned.

17 HENNESSY. And punished.

18 MITCHELL. Here here.

19 CARTER. He's been to court. It's all over and finished with.

20 MRS HENNESSY. You may think so.

21 CARTER. We have no way of proving that any of us wouldn't have acted the same way in his situation.

1 MITCHELL. You can't say that.

2 CARTER. I've a theory that I did say it.

3 HENNESSY. It doesn't hold water.

4 MITCHELL. It defies gravity.

5 HENNESSY. Because he did something . . . something dirty, yes dirty, I'm not afraid of the word. Because he did something dirty, you're saying we're dirty as well. And we haven't done anything . . . dirty.

6 CARTER. If you think you're so perfect, and whiter than white and close to God, that you can say . . . I am a better person than you, Edward Briggs . . . go ahead and say it . . . [Pause.] I'm not prepared to say that. I have no right to say that.

7 MITCHELL. There's got to be a difference between right and wrong. He was wrong to do what he did. And we're right to say he was wrong.

8 CARTER. He said so himself.

9 MITCHELL. Right.

10 MRS HENNESSY. Briggs will have to be watched.

11 AMY. Watched?

12 MRS HENNESSY. Yes. Watched.

13 AMY. What for?

14 MRS HENNESSY. Watched . . . for tendencies . . .

15 CARTER. The magistrate didn't consider it necessary to punish him.

16 HENNESSY. The magistrate said go away and keep your hands to yourself . . . but if you step out of line, we'll make you suffer for it . . .

17 MRS HENNESSY. We should do the same.

18 CARTER. I'm sure you will . . .

19 MRS HENNESSY. Watched. That's what he'll have to be.

20 CARTER. I'm simply trying to point out the Christian approach to the problem.

1   MRS HENNESSY. I've been a Christian rather longer than you have, Mr Carter . . .

2   AMY. You don't go to Heaven for good attendance.

3   MRS HENNESSY. That'll do, Amy.

4   HENNESSY. We've had experience of life, my dear.

5   MRS HENNESSY. And I'll please myself about Mr Briggs. If I think I want to speak to him, I will. If I decide not to, I won't. Either way, I'll decide. Not him. Me. [*Pause.*] And now, if we could have the hymn, I think it's time we went home.

A long pause. Then CARTER *gets up, slowly walks across to the piano. Strikes a single note. They sing.*

6   ALL. I will climb the City Wall,
I will see the Pastures Green,
I will drink the Nectar Sweet,
He will make me clean.
I will climb, I will see,
I will drink the Nectar.

As they sing, BRIGGS *comes in.*

I will climb the Mountain Top,
I will see the Promised Land,
I will drink the Waters Bright,
He will touch my hand.
I will climb, I will see,
I will drink the Waters.

They slowly become aware that BRIGGS *is in the room. One by one, they stop singing, a faltering stumble to a halt in mid-verse.*

I will climb to Calvary,
I will see the Crosses Three,
I will drink the Holy Wine,
He will smile at me . . .

The last line sung solo by MITCHELL. BRIGGS *smiles at him uncertainly, then at the rest of them.*

7   BRIGGS. I rang but nobody . . . because of the singing, I hope you don't mind . . . just walked in . . .

1 CARTER. That's perfectly all right.

2 MRS HENNESSY. We shall have to rush.

3 HENNESSY. Yes. Work to be done.

4 MRS HENNESSY. Always work to be done.

5 MITCHELL. I'll have to be off as well . . . my wife's not been too
    grand.

6 CARTER. Work to do? [*He challenges* HENNESSY.]

7 HENNESSY. It's my er . . . year end.

8 AMY. In June?

9 CARTER. The retail trade doesn't have years like other people
    have years.

10 MRS HENNESSY. Would you like a lift, dear?

11 AMY. No thank you, I'll walk.

12 HENNESSY. Are you sure?

13 AMY. I'll walk.

14 MITCHELL. Be careful, there's some . . .

    Pause

15 AMY. Some what?

    Pause.

16 MITCHELL. Well just . . . some . . .

17 MRS HENNESSY. Some funny people about.

18 AMY. Not really.

19 CARTER. Not really, no.

    Pause.

20 MRS HENNESSY. Goodnight Mr Carter.

21 HENNESSY. Goodnight Mr Carter.

22 CARTER. Goodnight Mr Hennessy, Mrs Hennessy. God bless
    you both.

23 MITCHELL. Goodnight Mr Carter.

24 CARTER. Goodnight Mr Mitchell. The Lord's blessing on your
    wife and your vehicle.

1 MRS HENNESSY. Goodnight Amy.

2 HENNESSY. Goodnight Amy.

3 MITCHELL. Goodnight Amy.

4 AMY. Goodnight. [*She turns very deliberately to* BRIGGS.] Goodnight, Mr Briggs.

5 BRIGGS. Goodnight.

> HENNESSY, MRS HENNESSY *and* MITCHELL *go out. A pause, then* AMY *follows them.*

> Am I too late for the meeting?

6 CARTER. I haven't formally closed it, as it happens.

7 BRIGGS. I see.

8 CARTER. We're still on any other business.

9 BRIGGS. That's for me. Any other business. [*Pause.*] There are some funny people about.

> *Fade to blackout.*

ACT TWO

BRIGGS *and* CARTER, *as before.*

10 BRIGGS. I'm sorry I was late.

11 CARTER. Late?

12 BRIGGS. For the committee meeting.

13 CARTER. It's not important.

14 BRIGGS. Punctuality is important. Never been late for a committee meeting ever.

15 CARTER. You weren't late.

16 BRIGGS. Half past seven you start. I was late. Officially.

17 CARTER. Officially.

18 BRIGGS. I was late. I'm sorry. Always giving lectures to the Youth Club about that. But they don't listen. Do it at the start of the evening, half of them aren't there yet.

Do it at the end of the evening, they all start rushing off. [*Pause.*] Do you think I drive people away?

2 CARTER. Of course not.

3 BRIGGS. I emptied this room very quickly.

4 CARTER. They know not what they do.

5 BRIGGS. Oh I forgive them, I forgive them all right. No worries on that score. I've got some . . . got some other business.

6 CARTER. Other business?

7 BRIGGS. You said you're still on any other business, officially.

8 CARTER. Officially, yes.

9 BRIGGS. I've got some.

10 CARTER. The floor is yours.

11 BRIGGS. Well you can guess can't you?

12 CARTER. I suppose so.

13 BRIGGS. I'd like to discuss . . . what I did. [*Pause.*] It was the same on Sunday.

14 CARTER. What was the same?

15 BRIGGS. People not speaking, looking the other way.

16 CARTER. They'll get over it.

17 BRIGGS. Like that song.

18 CARTER. Song?

19 BRIGGS. Where e'er you walk, people get out of the way. And at work. In the office.

20 CARTER. They get out of the way?

21 BRIGGS. No they speak and everything, except when you're the other side of the room. Then you hear them giggling. That's worse, the giggling.

22 CARTER. Not to worry. At least you haven't had anonymous phone calls. [*Pause.* CARTER *notices* BRIGGS's *reaction.*] You have?

23 BRIGGS. From people, I don't know who. Keep your filthy hands to yourself you dirty . . . bastard, one of them said,

sorry about the language Mr Carter, but that was the word, one of the words.

2   CARTER. Have you informed the police?

3   BRIGGS. No.

4   CARTER. It's an offence, ringing people up like that.

5   BRIGGS. What I did's an offence.

6   CARTER. All over and done with . . .

7   BRIGGS. But if the police like did anything about it and it went to Court it'd all be in the papers again, there'd only be more giggling and more not talking and more getting out of the way.

8   CARTER. If the phone calls continue, you should inform the police.

9   BRIGGS. I don't think I like the police. I respect them for what they do but I don't think I like them. Not now.

        Pause.

10   CARTER. Did you recognize the voices?

11   BRIGGS. Voices? What voices?

12   CARTER. The people ringing you up.

13   BRIGGS. No.

14   CARTER. Male or female.

15   BRIGGS. Various.

16   CARTER. No theories?

17   BRIGGS. No.

18   CARTER. Did it sound like anybody in the church?

19   BRIGGS. They wouldn't do that. Who'd be likely to do that?

20   CARTER. It has been known to happen.

21   BRIGGS. You mean regular church-goers turn out to be per-verts, filthy bastards, oh yes, I know about that, there was one in the paper only last week. [*Pause.*] I walked about for an hour.

22   CARTER. Tonight?

1   BRIGGS. Yes. Over an hour, walking about.

2   CARTER. It's a pleasant night.

3   BRIGGS. Promised myself the walk, across for the committee meeting. Saw the cars outside . . . Hennessy's car . . . Mitchell's mini-van . . . couldn't somehow carry on walking up the path, with them all here, after them not speaking and looking sideways on Sunday. Went in the park instead.

4   CARTER. Probably more fun than the committee meeting.

5   BRIGGS. Walked about for a bit. Then I sat down. Like a rest. I never realized it was near the tennis courts.

    Pause.

6   CARTER. I don't quite understand.

7   BRIGGS. I mean I didn't know it was near the tennis courts. It was just a seat. For sitting on. So I sat on it.

8   CARTER. Yes.

9   BRIGGS. And young Lennie Tanner walked past, you know him? Youth Club. Bit sort of . . .

10   CARTER. Flash Harry.

11   BRIGGS. Overconfident.

12   CARTER. I know Tanner, yes.

13   BRIGGS. Walking past and he said, Wotcher Briggsy . . . you know, he's . . .

14   CARTER. Overconfident.

15   BRIGGS. Wotcher Briggsy . . . watching the tennis then?

16   CARTER. I'm sorry. I don't see anything . . .

17   BRIGGS. I mean I was just staring into thin air, looking at nothing, the way you do. But he thought I was watching the tennis.

18   CARTER. Lots of people watch tennis. Thousands at Wimbledon . . . socially very desirable.

19   BRIGGS. There were some girls playing tennis. Some lads as well but also some girls in . . . shorts, like tennis things

and he thought, Tanner thought that I was watching them. Watching the girls.

2 CARTER. There's still nothing wrong in that. I wouldn't mind having a look myself some time.

3 BRIGGS. No good joking. I am a man who sits on a seat in the public park, watching girls play tennis. [*Pause.*] Obviously I couldn't sit there any longer. So I came along here to the committee meeting. Drove them away.

4 CARTER. Things to talk about.

5 BRIGGS. It would have been perfectly all right, watching tennis in the park, before Windermere. Not since Windermere. Things change.

6 CARTER. Tell me about Windermere.

7 BRIGGS. It was formed by glaciation . . .

8 CARTER. Not that. About what happened. You and Linda.

9 BRIGGS. You were in the Court. You heard it all.

10 CARTER. I heard some half-truths that passed for justice in action.

BRIGGS *almost laughs.*

11 BRIGGS. The alleged offence.

12 CARTER. I never alleged it was an offence.

13 BRIGGS. The eggs by the lake.

14 CARTER. You mentioned them in your lecture, didn't you?

15 BRIGGS. I did a lot of walking, on my own. Young people, they seem to want you out of the way a good deal . . . more than they used to a few years ago . . . so I'd walk. On my own. Found these eggs in a nest by the lake, and I tried to persuade some of the young people to come and have a look at them. Two or three occasions I said but they wouldn't come. Until the last night. [*He looks at* CARTER, *a little uncertain.*] Can I tell you?

16 CARTER. Tell me. It's a compliment to me.

17 BRIGGS. On the last night. I said who's coming to see the

eggs? And there was a bit of a laugh, as usual, then Linda Mitchell said ...

LINDA's *voice offstage.*

2 LINDA. Yes, I'll come and have a look.

3 BRIGGS. So across the fields and through the trees, down to the water. It was the day we'd been swimming, the day *they'd* been swimming, and she didn't say anything for a long time and then she said ...

A spot on LINDA, *standing quite still, away from* BRIGGS. *No movement, no physical contact, now or at any time in the sequence.*

4 LINDA. Took a lot of photos didn't you? Of all of us.

5 BRIGGS. It's nice for your parents, so they can see you had a good time.

6 LINDA. Suppose so.

7 BRIGGS. Might even give a talk to the Friday Fellowship, when I get the photos back from the chemist's.

8 LINDA. Yes, you do that.

Pause.

9 BRIGGS. Saw the eggs in the nest, she wasn't very interested so back we walked, away from the water, through the trees, more slowly, coming in dusk. And she's walking closer now, and says ...

10 LINDA. You looked embarrassed with all us girls, not much on, like you were hiding behind the camera, like hiding scared to come out.

11 BRIGGS. Not really no.

12 LINDA. Not used to seeing a girl like that?

13 BRIGGS. Not really, no.

14 LINDA. You wouldn't, being a good man. Bet you've never even touched a girl. You being a good man.

15 BRIGGS. Not really no.

16 LINDA. Doesn't hurt, doesn't hurt at all. Doesn't hurt the

man. Doesn't hurt the girl. Especially if he's a good man. [*Pause.*] Doesn't hurt, Mr Briggs.

Pause.

2 BRIGGS. And she took my hand. Like that, and . . . like that.

Each re-enacts the moment. Not touching. Just memory as she takes his hand and places it on her breast.

That's all.

They drop their hands, stand normally.

Walking back across the field, not touching, not speaking, just walking. That's all.

The lighting reverts to normal. LINDA *has gone.*

3 BRIGGS. It was good.

4 CARTER. I'm sure.

5 BRIGGS. Not dirty. Gentle. Sharing.

6 CARTER. Communion.

7 BRIGGS. What?

8 CARTER. An act of communion.

9 BRIGGS. That's a funny word to use.

10 CARTER. You didn't mention any of this in Court.

11 BRIGGS. You can't. Talking about it, makes it sound . . . silly. You'd only get the giggling and the walking away. [*Pause.*] She rang me up.

12 CARTER. Linda?

13 BRIGGS. Said she was sorry, for talking about it. Said she'd . . . keep the secret.

14 CARTER. Have you seen her since?

15 BRIGGS. Oh no, it wouldn't be right.

16 CARTER. If it was all right then . . .?

17 BRIGGS. She's seventeen, I'm past forty, it wouldn't be right. In any case she's what my father used to say like no better than she ought to be. You know?

1 CARTER. The biggest cow in the parish . . . to quote Lennie Tanner.

2 BRIGGS. It's ridiculous. [*Pause.*] I'm resigning from everything.

3 CARTER. Resigning from what?

4 BRIGGS. Chairman of the committee, Youth Club leader, all of it.

5 CARTER. There's no need.

6 BRIGGS. There is. There is need. Tend the flowers, make them grow, you said that.

7 CARTER. When did I say that?

8 BRIGGS. One of your sermons, when you first came here. You said the church should teach people how to lead full lives. Use all the muscles. Tend the flowers, make them, no, I said that already.

9 CARTER. They stick you in a pulpit, you've got to say something.

10 BRIGGS. I'm past forty and not a flower in sight. Not one.

11 CARTER. You can't blame the church for that.

12 BRIGGS. I can. I do.

13 CARTER. If God intended . . .

14 BRIGGS [*breaks in*]. There's nothing wrong with God. It's the people running him.

15 CARTER. I agree with you there. But . . .

16 BRIGGS. He was here thirty-four years the Reverend Bradley.

17 CARTER. That's a lot of marmalade.

18 BRIGGS. My parents thought he was God. Don't know who they thought God was but . . . I had the lot, right from being a lad. Jumble sales, church teas, Sunday School. Me, eight years old, Sunday School Anniversary concert . . . [*He recites, mechanically.*]
My Father takes care of me all through the day,
To make my feet always to walk in Thy Way.
Bless those who are sick and bless those who are sad,
And please let me help them, to make them feel glad.

[*Pause.*] Amen. That was my bit. Never forgot it. I forgot it at the time, my mother had to shout the words at me from the third row. Never forgot. Never mind, says Bradley afterwards, he's a good boy. He would never forget on purpose.

2 CARTER. And now you're a good man.

3 BRIGGS. By listening to the Reverend Bradley. Some things were good and some things were sinful. Hanging round street corners was sinful. Hanging round street corners with girls was very sinful. Smoking was sinful. Drinking was very sinful. Singing was a bit sinful, unless it was hymns. [*Pause.*] I walked past the Five Bells on the way here.

4 CARTER. The pub?

5 BRIGGS. Do you know it?

6 CARTER. I pop in now and again. My wife sometimes has committee meetings in the Singing Room.

7 BRIGGS. You hear them in the Five Bells. Singing and laughing and shouting. Smoking and drinking I daresay. A sinful noise, according to the Reverend Bradley, but it doesn't sound all that terrible. Sounds like a good noise. You don't hear noises like that in church. Always half-hearted . . .

8 CARTER. The flowers don't grow.

9 BRIGGS. Do they fight?

10 CARTER. Who?

11 BRIGGS. The people in the Five Bells.

12 CARTER. Hardly ever. You get more fights in church.

13 BRIGGS. Not with fists . . .

14 CARTER. Not now but I know a man overturned the tables, threw out the merchants and the moneylenders . . .

15 BRIGGS. If I was to start going into pubs now . . . after Windermere . . .

16 CARTER. It wouldn't matter at all.

17 BRIGGS. People . . .

1 CARTER. Forget about people. Come in with me some time.

2 BRIGGS. No point.

3 CARTER. Play you best of five at darts.

4 BRIGGS. I don't like beer, it'd be a waste of time going into a pub.

5 CARTER. You're not forced to drink beer.

6 BRIGGS. I get the sensation that to derive the maximum benefit from going into pubs, it's best if you like beer.

7 CARTER. How do you know you don't like beer?

8 BRIGGS. Well I've never actually tried it. But I've always been told I wouldn't like it.

9 CARTER. Try it.

10 BRIGGS. I never go into pubs.

11 CARTER. Buy some from an off-licence.

12 BRIGGS. I'd be frightened.

13 CARTER. Frightened?

14 BRIGGS. Frightened to ask, in case I asked for the wrong thing.

15 CARTER. Just say . . . a bottle of beer please.

16 BRIGGS. You've still got the problem of carrying it away . . . away from the shop.

17 CARTER. Somebody might see?

18 BRIGGS. Yes.

19 CARTER. You look them straight in the eye and say: I've just been in that shop for a bottle of beer.

20 BRIGGS. I wouldn't find that easy, Mr Carter. I suppose I'm making things difficult.

CARTER *goes to a cupboard. Brings out a bottle of beer and two glasses.*

21 CARTER. Let's make it easy.

CARTER *pours out two glasses. Gives one to* BRIGGS *who smells it cautiously.*

22 BRIGGS. That's like the smell as you walk past the Five Bells.

23 CARTER. Try it.

1 BRIGGS. I'll pay you for what I drink.

   Pause.

2 CARTER. He made the water into wine.

3 BRIGGS. What did he make the beer into?

4 CARTER. Call it communion.

   A reaction from BRIGGS, *then he takes a cautious sip. No facial change. A long, long pause.*

5 BRIGGS. It's . . . horrible.

6 CARTER. Some people have to persevere. I did . . .

7 BRIGGS. Acquired taste.

8 CARTER. Yes.

9 BRIGGS. I'm sorry.

10 CARTER. Don't apologize, no need . . .

11 BRIGGS. But I don't see what all the fuss is about.

12 CARTER. I'm not making a fuss, Mr Briggs.

13 BRIGGS. Going to all that bother to discourage people. Just let them taste it, that'll discourage them. It's . . . well, I can't explain, just . . . horrible. [*Pause.*] I'll leave the rest if you don't mind.

14 CARTER. Don't worry, I'll give it to the canary.

15 BRIGGS. I'm like the rest of them. All of them on the committee.

16 CARTER. You're not at all like them.

17 BRIGGS. We've all got bits missing. Flowers that never grew up.

18 CARTER. We're all like that.

19 BRIGGS. You can buy a bottle of beer. You can talk to the Youth Club without them giggling behind their hands. You've got a wife, and a child, it'll all carry on after . . . [*Pause.*] Not with me. Full stop. They might put it in the paper if I arrange it beforehand with the vicar or somebody. Oh yes, they'll say, old Briggsy, funny bloke, lived on his own. There was that bit of trouble with a young

144

girl . . . years ago now . . . and then they'll turn to the sports page. [*Pause.*] Bits missing. Like an old meccano set that's been stuck at the back of a cupboard for thirty years. Anything that's not missing is rusted.

2 CARTER. So let the church help, that's what we're here for.

3 BRIGGS. The church?

4 CARTER. People who are all adjusted and happy, they're no use to us . . . they're welcome but . . .

5 BRIGGS. You really cater for the nut-cases.

6 CARTER. That's not what I mean.

7 BRIGGS. The power of prayer? I can pray at home in my own little room. Then nobody can listen . . .

8 CARTER. We can pray together.

9 BRIGGS. On Sunday and you said let us pray so we prayed. And I looked along at Mrs Hennessy and she looked at me. And she said, without saying anything, I'm not praying for the likes of you. And I looked back and said, without saying anything, I'm not praying for the likes of *you*, Mrs Hennessy. That's your church, Mr Carter. Everybody praying like mad for number one.

10 CARTER. So we'll have to do better.

11 BRIGGS. It's no good. [*Pause.*] I thought you'd be more help.

12 CARTER. Tell me what you want me to do.

13 BRIGGS. I don't know. I think I want you to tell me I'm wicked and sinful, but if I work hard and pray hard maybe God will forgive me . . . eventually.

14 CARTER. You haven't been wicked and sinful.

15 BRIGGS. Everybody else thinks so.

16 CARTER. You're the victim of a set of circumstances, that's all. You behaved very sensibly. Lots of men would have tried to take advantage of Linda's generosity.

17 BRIGGS [*harsh*]. It's no good talking like that!

18 CARTER. It doesn't make sense, trying to be a martyr.

19 BRIGGS. No good trying to be a saint.

1 CARTER. It's not as if you tried to rape the girl.

   Pause. BRIGGS *is shaken.*

2 BRIGGS. I'm ... astonished that you should even consider such a possibility. I mean ... the difference in ages and ...

3 CARTER. I'm on your side, Mr Briggs.

4 BRIGGS [*shaking head*]. No. That's just the trouble. I get the impression you're on everybody's side.

5 CARTER. That's right. I am.

6 BRIGGS. That's no good.

7 CARTER. I thought that was my job.

8 BRIGGS. The old Reverend Bradley, he once caught me smoking. Twelve I was. It was horrible, like beer, but he caught me and he told my father, and he belted me. They weren't on my side. They were on the other side. He belted me.

9 CARTER. That was stupid.

10 BRIGGS. And after I'd had the good hiding, then they forgave me.

11 CARTER. What's it got to do with Linda Mitchell?

12 BRIGGS. What I did was wrong.

13 CARTER. An act of communion.

14 BRIGGS. Just because something's quite nice it doesn't make it right. Sweets are nice but they make your teeth fall out.

15 CARTER. Your teeth will fall out anyway.

16 BRIGGS. I'm waiting for someone to condemn me.

17 CARTER. You heard the magistrate.

18 BRIGGS. He pretended to understand. In view of his previous good behaviour ... employer's references ... an inexplicable lapse ... promises it won't happen again.

19 CARTER. It's all true.

20 BRIGGS. All pretending to understand then turning away to giggle. [*Pause.*] Is there such a thing as right and wrong?

146

1 CARTER. Yes.

2 BRIGGS. So tell me not to do it again.

3 CARTER. No.

4 BRIGGS. Say it. Don't do it again, Mr Briggs.

5 CARTER. No.

6 BRIGGS. Jesus said to the woman taken in adultery . . . go now and sin no more . . .

7 CARTER. A set of circumstances.

8 BRIGGS. Jesus said . . .

9 CARTER. Jesus said to the woman, neither do I condemn thee. Neither do I condemn *thee*, Mr Briggs.

   Pause.

10 BRIGGS. Where do I go for God's judgment?

11 CARTER. You won't get it at this shop.

12 BRIGGS. I suppose you don't believe in him either.

13 CARTER. In a way I do.

14 BRIGGS. I bet he's grateful.

15 CARTER. Don't suppose he notices.

16 BRIGGS. He *is* punishing me.

17 CARTER. How?

18 BRIGGS. Lennie Tanner in the park. The sideways glances from Mrs Hennessy. The telephone calls.

19 CARTER. Agents of the Lord's anger?

20 BRIGGS. You can't prove they're not.

21 CARTER. And what about Linda Mitchell?

22 BRIGGS. What about her?

23 CARTER. When she laid your hand on her breast. An agent of the Lord's tenderness?

   Pause.

24 BRIGGS. Impossible.

25 CARTER. He moves in a mysterious way, they tell us.

1 BRIGGS. Not as mysterious as all that.

2 CARTER. Look. I'm sorry if I don't share your belief in the power of the Almighty, but I don't. I don't believe He can do anything.

3 BRIGGS. You what?

4 CARTER. I don't believe God can do anything.

5 BRIGGS. Not much of a God, your God, is he?

6 CARTER. Not on his own, no. He can't wave a magic wand and get rid of the submarines and Porton Down and Greek colonels and General Motors . . .

7 BRIGGS. The Reverend Bradley led me to think otherwise.

8 CARTER. There's starving kids in Africa, all waiting for some guy like Bradley's God to move in with the soup kitchens. They'd sing a few hymns if he asked them, even. The only trouble is, he won't.

9 BRIGGS. I need a God who can do something.

10 CARTER. There ain't no such person. I can do things. You can do things. He can't.

11 BRIGGS. You're a sort of heathen, aren't you?

12 CARTER. I'm a Christian.

13 BRIGGS. It's your job to believe in God and tell people the difference between right and wrong.

14 CARTER. It's my job to love my enemy.

15 BRIGGS. Like me.

16 CARTER. You're not my enemy.

17 BRIGGS. I met a Norwegian once. [*Pause.*] Over here, learning the language. Came to church, I suppose he was a good man, like me. I said things to him, carefully: Good evening. How are you? And then I'd try something more complicated. And he wouldn't understand. So I'd say it again . . . very clearly. Very slowly. And still he wouldn't understand. The more trouble I took, trying to speak slow and clear, the less he understood. I'm sorry, Mr Carter, but it was like talking to you.

148

1 CARTER. The important thing's to keep talking.

2 BRIGGS. I suppose so. [*A long silence.*] I said, the next meeting of the Friday Fellowship, the do-it-yourself meeting, I said I'd give you a few minutes on photography.

3 CARTER. Oh yes . . . I remember . . .

4 BRIGGS. I won't be able to.

5 CARTER. We'll fall back on Mrs Hennessy's homemade jam.

6 BRIGGS. I got the next reel back from the chemist's and they're all overexposed. Most of them. The rest are out of focus. [*He looks at his watch.*] But I won't come anyway.

7 CARTER. I hope you will.

8 BRIGGS. I'll have missed the halibut by now.

9 CARTER. Can I give you a lift?

10 BRIGGS. I promised myself the walk. I said to Mr Mitchell, why buy yourself a . . . [*The thought peters out.*] How much do I owe you for the beer?

11 CARTER. You owe me nothing.

12 BRIGGS. No but . . . it'll be spoilt . . . what I've left . . . all gone flat hasn't it?

13 CARTER. It doesn't matter at all.

CARTER *very firm.* BRIGGS *shrugs. A pause.*

14 BRIGGS. No. It doesn't, does it?

BRIGGS *goes out.* CARTER *follows so far, then stops. The sound of the door closing, quietly and respectfully.* CARTER *lights a cigarette and pours out some more beer into his glass. He draws on the cigarette.*

15 CARTER. If God intended me to smoke, He'd have provided me with a chimney in my head. [*He drinks from the glass.*] If God intended me to drink beer, He'd have provided me with a bottle opener on my lower lip. [*Pause.*] If God intended Edward Briggs to walk home He'd have provided fish and chip shops that stay open until midnight. [*Pause.*] If, and this relates to the previous question, God intended me to give Edward Briggs a lift, He'd have provided me with a driving licence and the ability to

drive. [*Pause.*] And if God intended me to save Edward
Briggs why didn't He make me clever enough to do it?
If God really isn't all that bothered about cigarettes,
bottled beer, fish and chips, Edward Briggs walking
home, my inability to drive, wouldn't that be too much
of a coincidence? [*He takes notebook, pen and bible and sits down
to prepare a sermon.*] If God intended me to produce a
dynamic sermon that would shape men's destinies and
breach the dams of bitterness and guilt, why didn't He
make me clever enough to do it? [*Pause.*] If God intended
my congregation, hereafter termed flock, to act upon
my words which are no less than His words, when will
it start to happen? [*Pause.*] If, and this relates to my previous question, God intended people to listen to my,
that is, His words, why doesn't He make them come
and listen in the first place? In the, as it were, Beginning
was, so to speak, the Word. [*Pause.*] If God intended the
churches to be full, why are they empty? [*Pause.*] If God
is happy that they be empty, why doesn't He wreck
them with a brace of well-chosen thunderbolts? Thus
releasing more land for private housing development,
petrol stations and the urban freeways. [*Pause.*] If, and
this relates to my previous two questions, God wanted
the Word to be spoken on the streets, wouldn't that be
too much of a coincidence? [*Pause.*] But if God wants
me to speak the Word on the streets, in the Five Bells,
on the tennis courts, outside and inside the fish and
chip shop, and by the gentle banks of Windermere,
why didn't He make me clever enough to do it? [*Pause.*]
If God makes sense, why doesn't He make some sense?
[*Pause.*] If God wants his flock to believe in Him, why
doesn't He believe in His flock? Or in me? [*Pause.*] If God
wants me to believe in Him, why doesn't He make me
clever enough to do it? [*Pause.*] If we're on our own, me
and the flock, wouldn't that be too much of a coincidence?

Quiet organ music building up. CARTER *stands and moves to a pulpit
position.*

If I'm on my own, why doesn't He make me clever enough? [*Pause.*] If God wants me to be clever enough one day, how long, oh Lord, how long, do I stay thick? [*Pause.*] If God intended me to prepare legible, articulate notes for a sermon, why did He create felt-nibbed pens with built-in obsolescence? [*He tosses the pen aside.*] And if God doesn't intend me to preach half-baked sermons to half-empty churches, what can He do to stop me?

CARTER *is now in the pulpit. We can see the congregation sitting in neat rows to one side.*

If He doesn't know or care, wouldn't that be too much of a coincidence?

The music builds up, the congregation rises, they sing.

2 ALL. I will climb the City Wall,
I will see the Pastures Green,
I will drink the Nectar Sweet,
He will make me clean.
I will climb, I will see,
I will drink the Nectar.

The congregation sits. CARTER *addresses them, and the audience.*

3 CARTER. I am taking as my text . . . a funny thing happened on my way to church this evening. [*Pause.*] I was walking along Empire Terrace, that beautiful urban complex, back-to-back and crumbling, where the sun never sets because it is never seen to rise, and there I beheld a small boy. He was crying. Why are you crying? I asked him. He looked at me, dabbing his tears with a thrice-used handkerchief. He replied: I am crying because my elephant is dead. I replied: Never mind, perhaps Daddy will buy you another elephant. It is, after all, an affluent age, with unemployment down to eight per cent, and export orders flooding in to J. Snelgrove and Sons, Manufacturing Joiners. Replied the boy: I'm not crying because my elephant is dead, I'm crying because I don't know how to bury the . . . elephant. [*Pause.*] He was crying because he did not know how to bury it. Now,

the question is, how many of *us* have elephants, dead or in the early stages of decay, and do not know how to bury them? Most of us, I imagine. How many of us don't even make the effort to bury them? How many are not even aware that the elephant is dead? Again, most of us, I imagine. [*Pause.*]

I have an elephant.

Thou hast an elephant.

He, she or it has an elephant.

We have some elephants.

You have some elephants.

They have some elephants. [*Pause.*]

Now many of us think we can resolve this problem by coming to church regularly. That we can thereby leave the elephant in a celestial cloakroom whence it will by miracle disappear. This, in my view, is not the case. It is in the nature of . . . Nature that whatever you deposit in a cloakroom as you come in, must be collected again as you go out. [*Pause.*]

I have an elephant.

Thou hast an elephant.

He, she or it has an elephant.

We have some elephants.

You have some elephants.

They have some elephants. [*Pause.*]

And I said to the boy, why are you weeping? And he said unto me, I am weeping because I cannot bury the dead. Will you please rise.

The congregation stands.

Number fifty-seven in the red-backed book, a hundred and three in the grey.

They sing.

2 ALL. I will climb the Mountain Top,
I will see the Promised Land,
I will drink the Waters Bright,
He will touch my hand.
I will climb, I will see,

I will drink the Waters.

2 CARTER. Let us pray.

Heads bowed.

Blessed are the generals, the admirals, the marshals of the air, for theirs is the Kingdom of Heaven. Lord hear our prayer.

3 ALL. And let our prayer come unto Thee.

4 CARTER. Blessed are they that lose the pools, are vanquished by bingo, diminished by the betting shops, betrayed by the mail order catalogue, and fail to remove unwanted hair, fat or regional accents as guaranteed by the moneylenders. For they shall be comforted. Lord hear our prayer.

5 ALL. And let our prayer come unto Thee.

6 CARTER. Blessed are the bishops and archbishops, the popes and cardinals, the majority shareholders, the executive material, the official receivers, the gnomes of Zurich, the fairies of Whitehall. For they shall inherit the earth. Lord hear our prayer.

7 ALL. And let our prayer come unto Thee.

8 CARTER. Blessed are they that hunger and thirst after let's say avocado pâté du maison then coq au vin meunière Maryland d'Enrico then crêpe suzette sorbet flambé à la Cyril Ray garnished with after eights, say ten quid a throw excluding wine. For they shall be filled. Lord hear our prayer.

9 ALL. And let our prayer come unto Thee.

10 CARTER. Blessed are the leader-writers, interviewers, motivational researchers, official observers, the fact-finders, insighters, ruthless probers, statistical analyzers, keen-eyed watchers and cold hard gazers. May they obtain mercy. Lord hear our prayer.

11 ALL. And let our prayer come unto Thee.

12 CARTER. Blessed are the absentee landlords, the hidden persuaders, the mysterious wealthy, the concealed

moonlighters, the nebulous carpetbaggers, the secret controllers, the faceless, the mindless, the soulless. For they shall see God. Lord hear our prayer.

2   ALL. And let our prayer come unto Thee.

3   CARTER. Blessed are the unilateralists, subject to reasonable safeguards, the non-proliferators, subject to reasonable safeguards, the total abolitionists, subject to reasonable safeguards, the stout believers in conventional weapons, subject to reasonable safeguards. For they shall be called the children of God. Lord hear our prayer.

But now only AMY *responds.*

4   AMY. And let our prayer come unto Thee.

5   CARTER. The poor in spirit.

6   AMY. They that mourn.

7   CARTER. The meek.

8   AMY. They that hunger and thirst.

9   CARTER. The merciful.

10   AMY. The pure in heart.

11   CARTER. The peacemakers.

And from the others, silent rejection.

And he said unto me, I am weeping because I cannot bury the dead.

They sing.

12   ALL. I will climb to Calvary,
I will see the Crosses Three,
I will drink the Holy Wine,
He will smile at me.
I will climb, I will see,
I will drink the Wine.
Amen.

13   CARTER. There will be a meeting of the church committee immediately after this service.

A quick change of lighting and atmosphere. CARTER *goes off.*

HENNESSY, MRS HENNESSY and MITCHELL are shown into the room by MRS CARTER.

1 MRS CARTER. Perhaps you'd like to find the most comfortable seats.

They sit down, in their traditional order of precedence.

2 MRS HENNESSY. Thank you.

3 HENNESSY. Thank you.

4 MITCHELL. Thank you.

An uneasy pause.

5 MRS CARTER. You're all in good time.

6 MITCHELL. It's always best.

7 MRS HENNESSY. We all came together tonight . . . in the new Cortina.

8 MRS CARTER. How very nice.

9 MITCHELL. Had a little spot of bother.

10 MRS CARTER. I see.

11 HENNESSY. But that's what friends are for.

12 MRS CARTER [*baffled*]. Yes. [*Pause.*] Something wrong with the mini-van?

13 MITCHELL. Track rod ends.

14 MRS CARTER. I've heard they can be very serious.

15 MITCHELL. Very serious.

16 MRS CARTER. And how is your wife?

17 MITCHELL. It seems to be moving away from her knees.

MRS CARTER *not sure whether this is good or bad.*

18 MRS CARTER. I see.

19 MITCHELL. The doctor says it's psychosomatic but I think she imagines half of it.

The doorbell rings. MRS CARTER *answers it.*

20 HENNESSY. Who will that be?

1 MITCHELL. Amy I suppose.

2 MRS HENNESSY. Oh dear.

3 MITCHELL. It's democracy.

4 HENNESSY. It's difficult.

5 MRS MITCHELL. Unfortunate.

6 HENNESSY. Not to mention . . . a certain party.

   AMY *comes in with* MRS CARTER.

7 MRS CARTER. There you are Amy, find yourself a comfortable
   seat.

   AMY *sits down on one of the remaining chairs, the least comfortable
   one.*

8 AMY. Good evening.

9 MITCHELL. Good evening Amy.

10 HENNESSY. Good evening Amy.

11 MRS HENNESSY. Good evening, my dear.

   Pause.

12 MRS CARTER. How are the . . . A . . . levels?

13 AMY. Not too bad. Only biology to go.

14 MRS CARTER. Biology's quite nice, once you get used to it.

   Pause. Awkward smiles.

15 AMY. How's your wife, Mr Mitchell?

16 MITCHELL. Track rod ends.

17 AMY. Oh. I'm sorry.

   CARTER *comes in, very cheerful.*

18 CARTER. Good evening everybody, sorry to keep you waiting,
   I lost the soap.

19 HENNESSY. It can be difficult.

20 CARTER [*as he sits in the Chairman's seat*]. I hope all's right with
   the world. Mini-vans?

21 MITCHELL. Something to be desired.

1 CARTER. The old thirty-three and a third?

2 HENNESSY. Money's tight, to be honest.

3 CARTER. O levels?

4 MRS CARTER. A levels.

5 AMY. Apart from biology.

6 CARTER. Well, let's count our blessings, one, two . . . [*counting on his fingers*] . . . no, hardly seems worth it.

7 MRS HENNESSY. Flowers.

   Pause.

8 CARTER. Yes, flowers are indeed a blessing, granting us their splendour and only a modest charge on the rates.

9 MRS HENNESSY. Mrs Millican.

10 CARTER. Ah.

11 MRS HENNESSY. Still not a word?

12 CARTER. Not even a solitary petal.

13 MRS HENNESSY. Something will have to be done or I daren't predict the consequences.

14 MRS CARTER. Perhaps you could discuss it under any other business.

15 CARTER. That seems a good suggestion, we'll have a full and frank interchange of opinion.

16 HENNESSY. Are you staying for the meeting, Mrs Carter?

17 MRS CARTER. I thought I would. I don't want to miss the fun.

18 MITCHELL. Fun?

19 HENNESSY. I hear you were in the shop yesterday.

20 MRS CARTER. I heard about your special offer of custard creams and came running.

21 HENNESSY. Lovely little baby, according to my shop-girl.

22 CARTER. We think very highly of our baby.

23 MRS HENNESSY. Didn't she say something else, dear?

24 HENNESSY. Yes . . . er something.

25 MRS HENNESSY. I thought she did.

Pause. MRS CARTER *and* CARTER *smile.*

1 MRS CARTER. Brown baby? Is that what she said?

2 MRS HENNESSY. That was it, yes.

3 HENNESSY. Lovely little baby she said.

4 MRS HENNESSY. They make beautiful babies.

5 MITCHELL. Adopted?

6 CARTER [*smiling*]. Usual sources, Mr Mitchell.

   Blank reactions. CARTER *proceeds.*

   Right. I declare open this meeting of the St Amber's church committee and call upon the Honorary Secretary to read the minutes of the last meeting.

   Pause.

7 MRS HENNESSY. I've done it again.

8 MRS CARTER. I didn't know you'd done it before.

9 HENNESSY. At the last meeting.

10 MRS CARTER. I'm sorry I missed it.

11 CARTER. If I might interject? I think Mrs Hennessy means she's left the minutes in her other bag. That being so, may I propose from the chair that we take them as read, that we accept them as a true and accurate record, and that I sign them, as it were, as such.

12 AMY. Yes.

13 MITCHELL. Good idea.

14 CARTER. Unanimously.

15 HENNESSY. We might put on record a request for a little more urgency and efficiency from the Hon. Sec?

16 CARTER. We'll ask the Honorary Secretary to record that in the minutes.

17 MRS HENNESSY [*still fumbling in her bag*]. Pardon?

18 CARTER. Treasurer's report.

19 MITCHELL. Pretty much unchanged. [*He checks in small pocket notebook.*] The columns read . . . nil, nil, nil, nil and er nil.

20 HENNESSY [*making notes*]. What is the final nil?

1   MITCHELL [*checking*]. Carried forward.

2   HENNESSY. I see.

3   CARTER. We thank the Honorary Treasurer for his continuous and energetic application to duty and accept his report . . . unanimously?

No dissenters.

Unanimously. Next. The Youth in Christ committee. Amy.

4   AMY. Well we're all getting to the end of G.C.E., thank goodness . . .

5   MRS HENNESSY. It's very hard for them.

6   AMY. And we had planned an illustrated lecture by Mr Briggs on Easter in the Lake District but . . .

7   HENNESSY. We understand.

8   MRS CARTER. You're not having the lecture?

9   AMY. The next lot of slides came out rotten.

10 CARTER. It's difficult to overcome rotten slides.

Pause.

11 AMY. That's the end of my report. Sorry it's . . .

12 CARTER. Thank you Amy. Which brings us to your favourite and mine . . . any other business. [*Pause.*] If there is no further business . . .

13 MRS HENNESSY. I think there is.

14 CARTER. Oh good. I like business.

Pause.

15 MRS HENNESSY. I think my husband wishes to speak.

16 HENNESSY. You mean . . . a certain matter?

MRS HENNESSY *nods.*

17 MITCHELL. Oh yes.

18 MRS CARTER. You've discussed it amongst yourselves?

19 MITCHELL. Oh no.

1 CARTER. What certain matter?

2 HENNESSY. Well I think it's fair to say that it springs from . . . your last sermon.

3 CARTER. I see.

4 MRS CARTER. You liked it so much you'd like a copy?

5 HENNESSY. Er . . . no.

6 MRS HENNESSY. No.

7 MITCHELL. No.

8 AMY. I liked it.

9 MRS HENNESSY. Hush.

10 HENNESSY. Being quite blunt about it, some people felt . . . not happy.

11 CARTER. About the sermon?

12 HENNESSY. Not happy.

13 MRS HENNESSY. Unhappy.

14 CARTER. Anything specific?

15 HENNESSY. Yes. Elephants.

16 MRS CARTER. Elephants?

17 HENNESSY. Mainly the elephants.

18 CARTER. They didn't like me talking about elephants in a sermon.

19 HENNESSY. I think there was no objection to mentioning elephants . . .

20 MITCHELL. As such.

21 HENNESSY. As such. But too many.

22 MRS HENNESSY. It was the regularity of the elephants.

23 CARTER. I don't understand that, at least I don't think I do, I mean I hope I don't.

24 HENNESSY. You used the word elephant twenty-two times. Roughly. Some would regard that as a shade excessive.

25 CARTER. Twenty-two?

26 MITCHELL. Nineteen, I made it.

1 CARTER. Shall we say twenty, it's a nice round figure.

2 AMY. For nice round elephants.

3 MRS HENNESSY. Hush.

4 CARTER. Let's say twenty elephants. If you say it was around that number, I'm sure it must have been. But I wasn't talking about elephants.

Pause.

5 HENNESSY. No?

6 CARTER. No.

7 MRS HENNESSY. Fancy.

8 HENNESSY. Sure?

9 CARTER. Yes.

10 MITCHELL. Well, to me, when somebody mentions elephants nineteen . . .

11 HENNESSY. Twenty-two . . .

12 CARTER. Twenty.

13 MITCHELL. Twenty times in just over six minutes, I tend to think he's talking about elephants.

14 CARTER. Well I wasn't talking about elephants in a real sense.

15 MITCHELL. Oh.

16 HENNESSY. What were you talking about in a real sense?

17 AMY. He was using elephants as a symbol.

18 CARTER. Exactly.

19 MRS CARTER. It's by far the best way to use them.

20 MITCHELL. And of course, I married into this church, I wasn't sort of born to it.

21 AMY. A symbol.

22 MRS HENNESSY. But it's all right for you dear, you're doing your O levels . . .

23 HENNESSY. A levels.

24 AMY. Yes.

25 MRS HENNESSY. You'll understand these things.

1 AMY. I'm not doing A levels in elephants.

A shriek of laughter from MRS CARTER.

2 CARTER. It was really in the nature of a parable.

3 MRS HENNESSY. But there must be plenty of real parables you could use.

4 HENNESSY. There's some in the bible, isn't there?

5 MRS CARTER. They do say so.

6 CARTER. Well I can't give a firm undertaking not to mention elephants in future, or any other beast of the field for that matter . . .

7 MRS CARTER. Or bird of the air?

8 AMY. Or fish that dwell under the sea?

9 MRS HENNESSY. Hush dear.

10 CARTER. But I'll try to mix them a bit, no more than twenty of each, say . . . is there any other any other business?

11 MRS HENNESSY. Yes.

12 CARTER. Yes?

13 MRS HENNESSY [*to* HENNESSY]. You.

14 HENNESSY. Me?

15 MRS HENNESSY. Yes.

16 HENNESSY. Again?

17 MRS HENNESSY. Yes.

Pause.

18 HENNESSY. No, you.

19 MRS HENNESSY. All right. Mr Carter, there has been a certain amount of talk to the effect that you are taking part in a certain event next Sunday.

20 MRS CARTER. He's coming to church, yes.

21 MRS HENNESSY. Apart from that.

22 HENNESSY. They say you are taking part in a certain march.

23 CARTER. A protest march.

1   HENNESSY. That's what they say.

2   CARTER. They are right.

3   MRS CARTER. Did they say what the march is about?

4   MRS HENNESSY. I don't remember.

5   CARTER. That's relevant, isn't it?

6   HENNESSY. They seemed to think it was something, well, extreme.

7   CARTER. And they disapprove?

8   HENNESSY. They do.

9   CARTER [to MITCHELL]. Do they?

10 MITCHELL. They're not too happy.

11 AMY. Do they believe in free speech?

12 HENNESSY. Everybody believes in free speech.

13 MITCHELL. I fought for it in the Home Guard.

14 MRS HENNESSY. It's the extremism we're concerned about.

15 MRS CARTER. We?

16 MRS HENNESSY. They, that is.

17 HENNESSY. No. Let's face it. We.

18 CARTER. How do you know I'm an extremist?

19 MRS HENNESSY. You're going to march.

20 HENNESSY. That's extreme.

21 CARTER. Girl Guides march.

22 MRS CARTER. Cubs and Brownies march.

23 CARTER. Elephants march.

24 MITCHELL. They don't.

25 AMY. When the circus comes to town.

26 HENNESSY. Not politically.

27 MRS HENNESSY. Vicars don't march.

28 HENNESSY. That's the thing.

29 MRS HENNESSY. And on a Sunday.

30 MITCHELL. Could be a traffic hazard.

1 MRS HENNESSY. Politics and Sundays should be kept separate.

2 CARTER. Well I'm not even sure I agree with the other marchers but I'll die for my right to march with them, I think. Whether I agree with them or not. Does that clarify the situation?

3 MRS CARTER. Admirably.

4 HENNESSY. We respect that. We respect your point of view.

5 MRS HENNESSY. But it's the people you'll be associating with.

6 CARTER. Like who?

7 HENNESSY. Well, for a start, the sort of people who go on marches.

8 MRS CARTER. Who for example? What people?

9 MRS HENNESSY. Well. Several people.

10 HENNESSY. With long hair.

11 MRS HENNESSY. Yes. With long hair.

12 CARTER. I haven't got long hair.

13 MRS CARTER. I have.

14 HENNESSY. There's others.

15 MITCHELL. I should think Harry Bainbridge is involved, isn't he?

16 CARTER. Deeply involved.

17 MRS CARTER. Up to the brim of his cloth cap.

18 MITCHELL. Well then. No names, no pack drill but . . .

19 CARTER. Harry Bainbridge hasn't got long hair.

20 AMY. No names, you said, but you said a name. [*anticipating* MRS HENNESSY] Hush.

21 HENNESSY. You don't have to have long hair to be noted.

22 MRS HENNESSY. And he's noted.

23 HENNESSY. I'll say he's noted.

24 MRS HENNESSY. He's a trade unionist.

25 MITCHELL. He organized that last one.

26 HENNESSY. And there was talk in the Chamber of Commerce

about *that* I can tell you. A letter drafted to the Town Council.

2 MRS HENNESSY. Did they reply?

3 HENNESSY. We didn't post it, as a protest against the two tier postal system.

4 MRS CARTER. It's killing the corner shop, the two tier postal system.

5 CARTER. That and the breathalyzer.

6 HENNESSY. I'm glad you're beginning to see things my way. You must see there are two sides to my point of view.

7 MRS HENNESSY. At least.

8 HENNESSY. So if you'd like to reconsider.

9 CARTER. Certainly. [*Long pause as he reconsiders.*] I've reconsidered.

10 MRS HENNESSY. I am pleased. Genuinely.

11 CARTER. And I'm still going. Right. Last call for any other business.

12 MRS HENNESSY. I think we've had enough business for one night.

13 CARTER. I have one small item, deep with implications.

14 MITCHELL. Pardon?

15 CARTER. I have had a complaint from a parishioner that he has been sent to Coventry. Not to mention anonymous phone calls.

16 MITCHELL. Who from?

17 CARTER. And overall insulting behaviour, none of which comes under the heading of Christianity.

18 MRS HENNESSY. Who made the complaint?

19 CARTER. He didn't actually complain. I am making the complaint on his behalf. Mr Briggs.

20 MRS HENNESSY. Oh him.

21 HENNESSY. Well I don't mind admitting, I haven't spoken to him since . . . a certain revelation.

22 MITCHELL. And you'll realize I'm in a difficult position here, what with Linda . . .

1 CARTER. We then that are strong ought to bear the infirmities of the weak.

2 MRS CARTER. That's rather good.

3 HENNESSY. I quite agree. What was it?

4 CARTER. It's from the bible.

5 AMY. St Paul to the Romans.

6 MRS CARTER. But he didn't post it as a protest against the two tier crucifixion system.

7 MITCHELL. I've forgotten what he said now.

8 CARTER. We then that are strong ought to bear the infirmities of the weak.

9 MRS HENNESSY. I don't see what that's got to do with Mr Briggs.

10 HENNESSY. He's certainly not strong.

11 CARTER. I mean it's our responsibility to help him.

12 MRS HENNESSY. We can hardly do that, he's left the church.

13 HENNESSY. Run away.

14 MITCHELL. I was tempted to stick one on him.

15 AMY. He's been driven out.

16 MRS HENNESSY. I didn't.

17 CARTER. Driven out.

18 HENNESSY. My wife doesn't even drive.

19 MRS CARTER. They drove him out.

20 CARTER. We.

21 MRS HENNESSY. And good riddance. Get thee behind me Satan. That's from the bible as well.

22 CARTER. You think Mr Briggs is Satan?

23 MRS HENNESSY. Well I'm no expert but . . .

24 CARTER. He's the most innocent person I know.

25 MITCHELL. Getaway.

26 HENNESSY. What does Mr Mitchell's daughter say?

27 CARTER. The same, I should imagine.

1 MRS HENNESSY. I suppose you think what happened . . . what he *did* . . . was good?

2 CARTER. Yes. The best thing that ever happened to Mr Briggs.

Pause.

3 HENNESSY. I can't believe what I'm hearing.

4 CARTER. You heard right. It was good.

5 MRS HENNESSY. I suppose you think everybody should do it.

6 MRS CARTER. Whoopee.

7 CARTER. I'm not saying everybody should do it.

8 MRS HENNESSY. We might not *want* to do it.

9 MRS CARTER. Tastes do vary.

10 CARTER. Yes, you're certainly missing something, folks, get yours today.

11 HENNESSY [*angrily*]. Shuttup!

12 CARTER. I've shut up. The floor is yours.

Pause.

13 HENNESSY. Mr Carter. I think I'm speaking for a number of people . . . a considerable number of people . . .

14 MRS CARTER. Speak for yourself, Mr Hennessy. Let other people speak for themselves. Speak for yourself.

15 HENNESSY. All right. I'll speak for myself. I don't expect the vicar to spend all his time insulting his most loyal supporters. Mutual respect, that's what we always had with the Reverend Bradley . . .

16 AMY. Speak for yourself.

17 MRS HENNESSY. He is. That was made perfectly clear, Amy.

18 HENNESSY. Hush. But all we get's sly digs and insults and jokes and elephants. And it can't go on.

19 CARTER. Go on.

20 HENNESSY. The way you go on, you'd think . . . we'd all got a few screws loose or something. Like not all there. A few bits missing, all of us.

1   CARTER. Right.

2   HENNESSY. That's what you think?

3   CARTER. Certainly. All of us. All incomplete.

4   MRS CARTER. Unscrew your leg, dear, show them.

5   CARTER. So we share. Linda Mitchell had a little love to spare
      for Mr Briggs. So she shared it.

6   MITCHELL. Please don't take my daughter's name in . . . er . . .

7   MRS CARTER. Vain?

8   MITCHELL. Spends hours in front of the mirror.

9   CARTER. We're all a bit balmy. But if we hold hands maybe
      we'll keep this side of the precipice.

10   HENNESSY. I've never held hands with anybody.

11   MRS HENNESSY. You seem to be obsessed with . . . touching,
      Mr Carter.

12   AMY. He doesn't mean holding hands, like holding hands.

13   MITCHELL. Like elephants.

14   AMY. A symbol.

15   MRS CARTER. Holding trunks, that's what he means.

16   HENNESSY. But there's something you're all forgetting.

17   CARTER. What are we forgetting?

18   HENNESSY. Who pays the piper?

         Pause. Total universal bafflement.

19   MITCHELL. What?

20   HENNESSY. What I'm saying is that any organization like a
      church has to be run like a business. There's income and
      expenditure. You can always get another vicar. But you
      can't get people to pay the bills.

21   CARTER. Ah.

22   MRS CARTER. To each according to his needs. From each
      according to his profit margins.

23   HENNESSY. I mean we hear a lot about the Youth Club. Well
      where did the table tennis table come from? A gift

from the Almighty? No. Paid for. Hard cash. And who supplied the brushes for painting the church parlour? And who got the paint for you? Twenty-five per cent off the grey gloss? Without that you'd only have been able to paint three of the walls. And who started off the belfry renovation appeal with a cash donation that has yet to be matched by any other parishioner?

2   CARTER. You, Mr Hennessy, I suppose?

3   HENNESSY. Yes, me, I suppose. I suppose it must be me.

4   CARTER. And no doubt you'll get the Chamber of Commerce certificate for services to God the Father, God the Son and God the Holy Ghost.

5   HENNESSY. I'm facing facts, it's time you did.

6   AMY. It is easier for a camel to go through the eye of a needle than for a rich man to enter into the kingdom of God.

7   MITCHELL. I don't think camels have anything to do with it·

8   AMY. It's in the bible.

9   MITCHELL. Maybe when that was written but not in this day and age.

10   CARTER. It might be better to leave the camel in the cloak-room with the elephants.

11   MRS HENNESSY. It isn't a laughing matter.

12   MRS CARTER. Who's laughing?

13   MRS HENNESSY. People don't like jokes.

14   CARTER. I like jokes.

15   HENNESSY. I don't mind a clean joke.

16   MITCHELL. I like that one that ends: I'm not doing it down here I'm doing it over there.

17   HENNESSY. But it's not your job to laugh at people.

18   CARTER. I know. My job's to love people. And I say that without laughing, Mr Hennessy.

19   MRS HENNESSY. I suppose you love Mr Briggs.

20   CARTER. Certainly.

21   HENNESSY. You've got funny taste, that's all I can say.

1   CARTER. You've got to have funny taste to love people. But it's what I'm supposed to do. It's my job. [*He moves round them all in turn. Starts with* MITCHELL.] It's my job to love the man who married into a church that's second in his heart only to his track rod ends. And I love him. [*To* MRS HENNESSY] It's my job to love a woman whose religion involves territorial battles with Mrs Millican over who grows, waters, prunes, cuts, arranges, hangs, draws, and quarters the flowers. And I love her. [*To* HENNESSY] It's my job to love a man who pours nought point one per cent of his instant cocoa profit into table tennis tables, thus acquiring gilt-edged voting shares in the Hereafter. And I love him. [*To* AMY] It's my job to love a girl who has a devotion to church duty out of all proportion to any sensible study of the circumstances. And I love her. [*To* MRS CARTER] It's my job to love my militant atheist wife and march with her in many directions. And I love her.

2   MRS CARTER. Well up to the national average, I'd say.

3   CARTER. And it's my job to love Henry Briggs, who lightly touches a girl on a part of her body not sanctioned by the Chamber of Commerce and the Lady Magistrate's League of Decency and finds himself crucified for it. [*Pause.*] All. Without exception. And if you don't like it . . .

      Pause.

4   HENNESSY. If we don't like it . . . what?

5   CARTER. I'll keep on trying.

6   HENNESSY. We don't like it.

7   CARTER. Is that a general feeling?

8   MRS HENNESSY. Yes.

9   MITCHELL. Well I er ought to abstain but . . .

10   CARTER. You don't like it.

11   MITCHELL. No.

12   AMY. I don't mind.

1 MRS HENNESSY. Hush Amy.

2 AMY. Hush yourself.

3 MRS CARTER. Good girl.

4 CARTER. I can't use my casting vote if the feeling of the meeting is against me. But I'd like it put on record, that I agree with myself. [*Pause.*] Don't worry. My letter of resignation is behind the clock, along with the electric bill and the Readers Digest subscription. Which sort of means there is no further business and I declare this meeting closed and bless all who sail in her.

The meeting takes a deep breath and pretends to relax.

5 MRS CARTER. Would anybody like coffee and homemade iced fancies?

6 HENNESSY. We'll have to dash I'm afraid, sorting out the books for the Chancellor, it's the year end, you see.

7 MRS CARTER. I never stand between the year and its end, Mr Hennessy.

8 MITCHELL. And I've got to call at the chemist's . . . prescription . . .

9 MRS CARTER. For your wife's knees?

10 MITCHELL. Be ready by now.

11 MRS HENNESSY. Are you ready Amy?

12 AMY. I'll walk.

13 MRS HENNESSY. Walk?

14 AMY. Walk. First one leg, then the other.

15 MRS HENNESSY. But it's dark and there's a perfectly good Cortina outside . . .

16 AMY. I'd rather walk.

    Pause.

17 MRS HENNESSY. Goodnight Mrs Carter. Goodnight Mr Carter.

18 MRS CARTER. Goodnight.

19 CARTER. Goodnight.

1 HENNESSY. Goodnight.

2 MITCHELL. Goodnight.

3 CARTER. Goodnight.

4 AMY. Goodnight.

> MITCHELL, HENNESSY *and* MRS HENNESSY *go out,* MRS CARTER *seeing them off.*

5 MRS CARTER [*off*]. God, there's my bloody iced fancies going up in smoke.

> *Pause.*

6 CARTER. There's a perfectly good Cortina outside.

7 AMY. Who needs it?

8 CARTER. Various shareholders think they're a good idea.

9 AMY. I just didn't want you to think I was with them.

10 CARTER. I know that. Often been going to tell you . . . don't let the Christians grind you down, but you seem to have found out for yourself.

11 AMY. Christians.

12 CARTER. I'd put that lot in an arena with the lions any day and watch out for flying manes.

13 AMY. Been telling the truth tonight, haven't we?

14 CARTER. It's been dribbling out here and there.

15 AMY. Devotion to the church you said.

16 CARTER. I said.

17 AMY. Not true.

18 CARTER. Not true?

19 AMY. Not to the church. More like personal.

20 CARTER. Like personal.

21 AMY. No other reason for coming to all these terrible meetings.

22 CARTER. I can see that.

23 AMY. Sorry to be so bloody silly.

1 CARTER. I've done lots of bloody sillier things.

2 AMY. But if you're going, I wanted you to know.

3 CARTER. Thank you. [*He kisses her gently on the cheek.*] Thank you for the elephant.

4 AMY. A magical act of communion, like between Linda and Mr Briggs.

5 CARTER. Was it?

6 AMY. A bit. Difficult, in front of all these people.

7 CARTER. Believe me, I'm tempted, but my wife's hosing down the iced fancies in the next room and . . .

8 AMY. Goodnight Mr Carter.

9 CARTER. Good luck with the biology.

10 AMY. Thank you.

11 CARTER. Thank you.

AMY *goes. A pause, then* MRS CARTER *comes in.*

12 MRS CARTER. A beautiful song, beautifully sung.

13 CARTER. Did you enjoy it?

14 MRS CARTER. They don't write scenes like that any more.

15 CARTER. Avowals of love aren't that thick on the ground, I can't ignore them.

16 MRS CARTER. And you're going to abandon ship?

17 CARTER. Yes. The cock crew a third time and race you to the lifeboat.

18 MRS CARTER. What will you do?

19 CARTER. Look in the New Statesman. Liberal situations vacant. [*He picks up a magazine, perhaps even the N.S.*] P.R.O. for the Salvation Army in Hampstead.

20 MRS CARTER. There's a place that needs salvation.

21 CARTER. Speaker finder for the anti-vivisectionists.

22 MRS CARTER. No luncheon vouchers.

23 CARTER. Do you think I could write social titbits for Black Dwarf?

1   MRS CARTER. I think you'll find you're not terribly good at anything.

2   CARTER. Correct. I'm not. And I've got to try.

3   MRS CARTER. Seriously though, folks.

4   CARTER. Seriously though. What were the twenty-two elephants doing outside Wembley Stadium?

5   MRS CARTER. I don't know. What were the twenty-two elephants doing outside Wembley Stadium?

6   CARTER. They were looking for a referee.

MRS CARTER *takes his letter of resignation from behind the clock.*

7   MRS CARTER. Why does your letter of resignation say best prices paid for old woollens?

8   CARTER. Because I haven't written the letter yet. Don't know whether you spell faith with an F or a PH. I'm a lousy vicar.

9   MRS CARTER. You don't seem to go down too well with your flock.

10   CARTER. Briggs said it all. In the good old Reverend Bradley days you had your deadly sins . . . right? Avarice, Pride, Lust, Capitalism, Come Dancing . . . whatever they were . . .

11   MRS CARTER. You could have them all in a night and still have change out of six pence.

12   CARTER. And you had your deadly virtues, and if the vicar caught you having a virtue you got a bag of sweets and if he caught you having a sin you got a bloody good hiding. Heaven or Hell, each way bet, no savers.

13   MRS CARTER. If you think it's good, preach it.

14   CARTER. I don't think it's any good at all. But he could say all his in two sentences. Me, I need twenty-six weekly programmes on B.B.C.2. [*Pause.*] I'm glad there's the march on Sunday or there'd be nothing to look forward to at all.

15   MRS CARTER. It's off.

16   CARTER. Have they stopped making the flagpoles?

1 MRS CARTER. No. Harry Bainbridge rang. The unions won't
   back the march. Too many of their people working
   on the flagpole contract. So the march would consist
   of me, you, Harry and the executive committee of the
   folk song club.

2 CARTER. Hairy Dan.

3 MRS CARTER. Hairy Dan.

4 CARTER. Not so much a protest march, more a group of
   friends out for a walk.

5 MRS CARTER. That's what it would look like. [*Pause.*] The
   unions would back a protest march about unemployment.

6 CARTER. Still eight per cent, same for three months.

7 MRS CARTER. The Ministry says that when the eight per cent
   is seasonally adjusted, we're over the hump.

   Pause.

8 CARTER. Pity about the march. It's good to have a focus.

9 MRS CARTER. Your letter of resignation, that's a focus.

10 CARTER. Yes, it is.

   Baby cries, off.

   There's another.

   MRS CARTER *goes off.*

11 CARTER. [*sitting down to write*]. The Bishop's Palace, P.O. Box
   1AA, Dewsbury. Dear Sir or Madam. With reference to
   yours of the ultimate . . . yours of the infinite . . . my
   fiancée and I have difficulty in restraining . . . [*Pause.*]
   While restraining ourselves on the banks of Windermere
   the first cuckoo stole an egg from a nest by the water. I
   enclose the cuckoo. [*He stands.*] A funny thing happened
   to me on my way to the Bishop's Palace tonight. I was
   walking past the flagpoles of Wembley Stadium when
   I saw twenty-two elephants holding trunks in protest.
   I asked their spokesman: what seems to be the trouble?
   He replied: we have shot our referee. Never mind, I said,

the Confederation of British Industry will get you another through the trade, but he shook his head. Alas said the spokesman, our problem is we cannot bury him. I hurried on, in case I met any more elephants.

A lighting change. One by one, during this sequence, we discover the other characters on stage: casual and not too formal.

Anyway, once I got here, I was just leaving my elephant in the cloakroom when the man at the door said . . .

2   MITCHELL. If you want a hand with that, I've got the van outside.

3   CARTER. Thank you, sir, I love you.

4   MITCHELL. I can tell you're having trouble with the legs.

5   CARTER. There's a lot of legs about.

6   MITCHELL. But they are a blessing.

7   CARTER. For walking mainly. And marching.

8   MRS HENNESSY. Aldermaston indeed.

9   CARTER. Indeed.

10   MRS HENNESSY. No wonder that elephant looks sick.

11   HENNESSY. I'll get you another one, through the trade.

12   CARTER. I love you too.

13   HENNESSY. Twenty per cent for cash.

14   MRS CARTER. And still have change out of six pence.

15   HENNESSY. You might have trouble burying that one.

16   LINDA. It doesn't hurt.

17   CARTER. I know a bishop, he'll give me twenty per cent.

18   MRS HENNESSY. You'll need somebody to do the flowers.

19   CARTER. Mrs Millican.

20   MRS HENNESSY. I'll have a word.

21   BRIGGS. You'll have to water the flowers, make them grow.

22   LINDA. Water from the lake.

23   BRIGGS. One of nature's many miracles, formed by glaciation.

1   AMY. It's all biology.

2   MRS CARTER. Continuity.

3   AMY. Difficult, biology.

4   CARTER. It's all we've got.

5   AMY. Continuity.

6   MRS CARTER. Generation to brown generation.

7   CARTER. Well, somebody's got to try. [*Pause.*] The pattern.

8   MITCHELL. The pain in the legs.

9   MRS HENNESSY. The flowers.

10   HENNESSY. The friend in the trade.

11   LINDA. The eggs by the river.

12   MRS CARTER. The protest.

13   BRIGGS. The giggling and walking away.

14   AMY. And a little love besides.

    Pause.

15   CARTER. Yes. All together.

    They say the Lord's Prayer, quietly, so that we scarcely hear the words. CARTER *does not join in.*

16   ALL. Our Father, which art in heaven. Hallowed be Thy name. Thy kingdom come, Thy will be done on earth, as it is in heaven. Give us this day our daily bread. And forgive us our trespasses, as we forgive those that trespass against us. And lead us not into temptation, but deliver us from evil. For Thine is the kingdom, the power and the glory, for ever and ever. [*Pause.*] Amen.

    Pause.

17   CARTER. And much good may it do you.

    Fade to blackout.

Seventeen Per Cent Said Push Off

A play for television

CHARACTERS

GAVIN
DAVE
MR MILNER
MRS MILNER
BETTY
TERRY
FRANK
KEN

Seventeen Per Cent Said Push Off

A BEDROOM IN THE MILNERS' HOUSE IN THE NORTH   Day

*In vision we explore the tight little bedroom of a working-class
terrace house, taking in the faded floral paper, the mature wardrobe
wedged between the wall and the bed end, and the occasional pin-
ups typical of a teenage lad—mainly footballers who were in vogue
two or three years ago. There are no girlie pictures but you can see
where they have been.*

On sound, we hear GAVIN's *voice, but we do not see his face. We may
glimpse his feet in the course of the visual exploration. The room is
clean as a new pin.* GAVIN's *voice is sound, middle-class Guildford
but in no sense soppy.*

1   GAVIN [*voice over*]. The room is nine feet long by seven feet
    wide ... note ... check and insert metric equivalents ...
    ceiling height is seven feet nine inches. The normal
    occupant of the room is the son of the house, David ...

THE MILNERS' LIVING-ROOM   Day

*The living-room downstairs. All we see at this moment is a close
up of* DAVE—*full title David Milner—a tough and cheerful extro-
vert, aged twenty, a semi-skilled labourer because apprenticeships
don't pay enough at school-leaving—but bright enough and resourceful
enough to master any manual craft if he set his mind to it. He grins
into the camera.*

2   DAVE. Everybody calls me Dave.

THE BEDROOM   Day

Now we see GAVIN—*full title Gavin Calder—lying on the bed,
talking into a hand-mike linked to a small cassette tape-recorder on a
bedside chair.* GAVIN *is an Oxbridge post-graduate in his early
twenties, a good-looking lad with longish hair, dressed expensively,
but casually, for these parts. He is friendly, earnest about his work,*

has a good line in charm, likes to be liked and hasn't a single original thought in his head. He continues to speak into the recorder.

1 GAVIN. Everybody appears to call him Dave. The room is extremely clean, the wallpaper is cheap, rather insipid and er . . . [*He pauses, unable to think of anything else to say about the wallpaper.*] My impressions of the parents can only be vague at this stage . . .

THE LIVING-ROOM Day

Now we look at the parents, MR and MRS MILNER, in the physical context of the living-room and the tiny kitchen adjoining. The living-room is small, this fact emphasized by the amount of furniture it contains: the dining table and chairs, sideboard, two armchairs and large black and white console T.V set. MRS MILNER is setting the table for what they call lunch in Guildford, dinner here. She is about fifty, with a good, humane face, a generous nature sometimes concealed by a brusque manner. As we look at her we hear GAVIN's voice.

2 GAVIN [*voice over*]. Mrs Milner appears to be a definitive working-class mother . . . Mam, as they say. I would say she is a good organizer and a good housekeeper, though I have no firm evidence at this moment . . .

MRS MILNER moves away from the table and goes through the open door that leads to the small kitchen/scullery adjoining. MR MILNER is washing himself at the sink. He is a year or two older than his wife, a quiet intelligent man—a fitter by trade.

. . . Her relationship with Mr Milner appears to be good and friendly.

3 MRS MILNER. Come on, get your fat carcase out the way . . .

MILNER, who is decidedly unfat, mumbles through the soap as he looks for the towel hanging on the back of the door.

There you are, helpless . . . [*She hands him the towel.*]

4 DAVE. Did you say helpless or hopeless?

DAVE sits in one of the armchairs reading a racing paper and smoking a woodbine. He guffaws, delighted with his joke.

THE BEDROOM   Day

GAVIN *continues to speak into the recorder.*

1   GAVIN. I have reached no firm conclusions about Mrs Milner
    as yet. Er . . . the family's attitude to me since I arrived
    this morning has been friendly, cooperative and totally
    unselfconscious. [*He looks at his watch.*] Saturday . . . five
    minutes to twelve . . . time for lunch . . . that's to say,
    dinner.

    He switches off the recorder, quite pleased with this last amendment.

THE LIVING-ROOM   Day

Now MILNER *sits opposite* DAVE, *in the other armchair, as* MRS
MILNER *finishes setting the table.*

2   DAVE. Soft sod, talks to himself.

3   MILNER. Maybe they do that in Oxford.

4   MRS MILNER. Just 'cause he's cleverer than you . . .

5   DAVE. I don't call it clever, talking to yourself . . . I call it soft.

6   MRS MILNER. Depends what he says.

7   MILNER. Depends what sort of answers he gets.

8   DAVE. I call that soft, an' all . . . [*Pause.*] Any road, I'll ask him
    what he's up to . . .

9   MRS MILNER. You'll do nothing of the sort . . .

10 DAVE. If he's having my room tonight . . .

11 MRS MILNER. This week . . .

    She says it quietly so the reality doesn't dawn on DAVE *immediately.*

12 DAVE. I want to know what he's doing up there. [*Then it dawns.*]
    This week?

13 MRS MILNER. He might stay a few days . . .

14 DAVE. Bloodyell.

    MILNER *has a quiet chuckle to himself.*

    All right for you, you're not sleeping down here . . .
    flaming professors.

183

GAVIN comes into the room, smiling and bland.

1 GAVIN [*to* MRS MILNER]. You said I had to be down by twelve . . .

2 MRS MILNER. Aye, it'll just be a few minutes . . . sit yourself by the fire . . . Dave . . .

The last is an instruction to DAVE *to give his chair to* GAVIN. DAVE *shrugs then gets up and offers the seat with a dour politeness.*

3 GAVIN. There's no need . . .

4 DAVE [*an order*]. Sit down.

GAVIN sits down. DAVE *moves round the table to the sideboard.*

I enjoy leaning on the sideboard.

MRS MILNER, *still commuting between table and kitchen, looks daggers at* DAVE.

5 MRS MILNER. Is your room all right love?

6 GAVIN. Yes, thank you, Mrs Milner . . . super.

7 DAVE. Cig?

8 GAVIN. No thank you, I don't.

DAVE *lights another.*

9 MRS MILNER. Neither should he.

10 DAVE. I've got to . . . stops me worrying about smoking. Hey . . . Gavin . . .

11 MRS MILNER. Be quiet . . . [*She fears the worst.*]

12 DAVE. Give over . . . I'm making conversation, aren't I? [*To* GAVIN] You don't mind do you?

13 GAVIN. Go ahead.

14 DAVE. Do you really talk to yourself?

Pause. GAVIN *is the least concerned of the lot, barring* DAVE.

15 GAVIN. Yes.

16 DAVE. That's all right then. Long as you know about it.

17 GAVIN. Actually, I was talking into a tape-recorder . . . I find it's quicker than making notes . . . when I'm on a research project . . .

1 DAVE. When you're on a what?

2 GAVIN. A research project.

3 DAVE. Never been on one of them. Been on a bike.

4 MILNER. What you researching into, son? Mam said something but it didn't make sense.

5 DAVE [*musing*]. Been on the big dipper. Been on the beer. Been on the dole.

6 GAVIN. I'm writing a post-graduate thesis called The Infrastructure of the Working Classes . . .

   Pause.

7 DAVE [*to* MILNER). Serves you right for asking.

8 MILNER. A thesis, that's like a book isn't it?

9 GAVIN [*cautiously*]. Yes. Initially it's for a Ph.D., but it could turn into a book later . . .

10 DAVE. You want to see what makes us tick?

11 GAVIN. That's about it, yes.

12 DAVE. You couldn't have come to a better place.

   There is a bang as the front door opens and shuts, footsteps in the tiny hallway, then BETTY *comes in. She is a bright, attractive, down-to-earth girl, a few years older than* GAVIN.

13 BETTY. Hello, Mam, just want to borrow some sugar . . .

14 DAVE [*to* GAVIN]. Always on the scrounge, get that down.

15 BETTY. Hello Dad, hello big mouth . . .

   To DAVE, *who aims a friendly punch at her head as she sees* GAVIN.

   Oh, is this him?

   MRS MILNER *comes through from the kitchen with the sugar.*

16 MRS MILNER. Yes, that's our Gavin.

   GAVIN *stands up.*

17 DAVE. Me big sister Betty.

18 GAVIN. Hello.

1 BETTY. Hello, love. Nice to meet you, don't bother to stand up . . . just bow.

2 DAVE. Watch her, she's sex mad.

3 MRS MILNER. Shuttup! [*She digs* DAVE *in the ribs, so that it hurts.*]

4 BETTY [*picking up the sugar*]. Thanks, Mam, I'll have to dash.

5 MRS MILNER. Have you heard from your Sid?

6 BETTY. Not for a week.

7 DAVE. He's got a woman.

8 BETTY. I shouldn't be surprised. Ta-ta then . . .

Her general farewell includes a friendly smile at GAVIN, *but nothing too pointed.*

9 MRS MILNER. Ta-ta love.

There is a chorus of ta-tas and a goodbye from GAVIN *as she goes out.*

Come to the table then.

The men move to the table.

10 MILNER. You sit there, lad . . .

11 GAVIN. Thank you.

12 DAVE. Will you carve or shall I, father?

DAVE *sends up* GAVIN's *accent, as* MRS MILNER *comes in with the plates and sets one down in front of* GAVIN, *one in front of* MILNER. *She goes off for the other two for* DAVE *and herself. Each plate contains a mighty down-to-earth meal of chops, mashed potato and veg.* GAVIN *is taken aback by the size of it.*

All right, kid?

13 GAVIN. Yes . . . fine. . .

14 DAVE. Skates on, you've only got five minutes.

15 GAVIN. Five minutes?

16 MRS MILNER. What you talking about?

17 DAVE. Taking him out, aren't I?

18 MRS MILNER. Are you?

1   GAVIN. Are you?

2   MILNER. God help him.

We briefly hold GAVIN's *reaction: mingled anticipation and apprehension, before cutting sharply to:*

THE STREET   Day

We see GAVIN *and* DAVE *come out of the house, one of a terrace leading onto the main street. They walk down the terrace and turn onto the main street—in itself a residential street; pre-1914 terrace houses punctuated with corner shops—not slum property but the kind of high density, decaying area that is found all over the industrial North—hard, warm and forgotten.*
DAVE *walks* GAVIN *quickly and cheerfully, aiming a kick at a ball some kids are larking with, in and around the pavement—with occasional trips on to the road. Against these images we hear* GAVIN's *voice over.*

3   GAVIN. There appears to be a clearly defined structure to Saturday afternoon. Lunch ... that is to say, dinner ... is eaten early and quickly so as not to waste, quote ... valuable drinking time ... unquote. As an outsider, one gets the feeling that one is treading a well-worn traditional path that stretches back through the generations.

They turn and walk into a building—a fairly severe, brick building—and we see the sign over the door: Cleveland Trade and Labour Club.

INSIDE THE CLUB   Day

DAVE *and* GAVIN *are standing in a group at the bar. The place looks much like a pub, except that the beer is cheaper, a point that is not visually apparent though they all tend to drink a lot. There is a dartboard, a notice board with posters about concerts, union meetings, and a display of dirty seaside postcards. The place is both full and noisy.*
DAVE's *chief mates are in the group.* TERRY, *a big brawny lad, slightly overweight,* KEN, *smaller and fitter—like a boxer, light or welterweight—and* FRANK, *dark-haired and snappy dresser, very likely sea-going. All three are about* DAVE's *age—early twenties. At this moment they are reacting to* GAVIN.

1 TERRY. Mucky book, is it?

2 FRANK. He likes owt like that.

3 KEN. Important subject is sex, needs books writing about it ...

4 TERRY. Women in Love, did you see it? Bloody Hell fire ...

5 DAVE. Belt up, you're embarrassing my Oxford friend ...

6 KEN [*to* GAVIN, *indicating* DAVE]. You want to watch him, he's
   bent.

7 TERRY. Kinky.

8 FRANK. Goes to work in men's clothes.

9 KEN. I mean, you don't know which way to turn do you?

10 DAVE. Come on, sup up ...

   GAVIN's *pint glass is still half full. The others are empty.*

11 GAVIN. I'm all right, thanks.

12 DAVE. Gerrit down you, kid ... [*He shouts across the bar.*] Five
   more please, Ted.

13 GAVIN. Well let me get them ...

14 DAVE. You're not a member.

15 KEN. Not every day we get a professor in here.

16 GAVIN [*shrugs*]. O.K. Thank you.

17 TERRY [*to* DAVE]. What you doing tonight, kid?

18 DAVE. The usual. Are you?

19 TERRY. Aye. [*He looks across at* KEN *and* FRANK.]

20 KEN. I reckon.

21 FRANK. I'll probably see you.

   A tray of pints is slid across the counter and DAVE *hands the tray
   round. Each of them takes a glass,* GAVIN *placing his on the counter
   behind him as he still has some beer left in his original glass.*

22 GAVIN. What do you usually do on a Saturday night?

   They all laugh.

23 TERRY. The usual.

1　KEN. You know.

2　FRANK. What everybody does.

3　DAVE. Mind you, it doesn't half chafe your elbows.

> *Another explosion of laughter. The laughter fades and we lose natural sound and hold a close shot of* GAVIN, *then slowly tilting to his hand as it takes another pint from another tray and quietly slides it on to the counter behind him, beside the other glass, which is also still full. Over this we hear his voice.*

4　GAVIN. Their speech patterns are colourful, liberally punctuated with swear words and quasi-obscenities, though whether they moderated or exaggerated this for my benefit I don't know. Sex appears to be a major topic of conversation.

> *We cut away from the shot of the two glasses, picking up natural sound as* FRANK *is in the middle of an epic account of a recent nocturnal encounter.*

5　FRANK. And then she says No . . . just like that . . .

6　TERRY. She must have had another look.

7　FRANK. What's up, I says . . . the cat's watching, she says . . .

8　DAVE. Give over . . .

9　FRANK. Can't do it, she says, not with the cat watching . . .

10　KEN. Don't believe a flaming word.

11　FRANK. Honest, kid. . .

12　KEN. Lying hound.

13　FRANK. She says . . . I never can do it when the cat's watching . . .

> *Another eruption of laughter and again we lose natural sound and see a close shot of* GAVIN *before we watch him take another pint off another tray and place it on the counter. Now there are three pints in a row on the counter as we hear* GAVIN's *voice over the whole of the sequence.*

14　GAVIN. There are tantalizing gaps in the anecdotes, but the general theme is that of the storyteller in the role of the aggressor.

We cut from the glasses and pick up natural sound as KEN *is in the middle of the story of a recent triumph.*

1   KEN. So I give him one on the nose . . .

2   DAVE. Aye.

3   KEN. Then I give him another one in the guts . . .

4   TERRY. Good lad.

5   KEN. Then what?

6   FRANK. What?

7   KEN. Eddie come out into the yard and told me it was the wrong feller . . .

8   DAVE. The wrong feller?

9   KEN. Aye.

10   TERRY. And you're belting him?

11   KEN. And it's the wrong feller.

12   DAVE. What did you do then?

13   KEN. Well we had a bit of a laugh about it . . .

14   TERRY. Bet he was laughing, the one you'd been thump-ing . . .

15   KEN. Oh aye, couldn't stop.

Another mutual guffaw. Again we see GAVIN—*eyes a little glazed now*—*and again we see him trying to sneak the pint on to the counter. We hear his voice over.*

16   GAVIN. The herd instinct is very strong. Everybody speaks and drinks and behaves according to unwritten laws and it is unusual for anybody to break the rules.

TERRY sees GAVIN'*s row of pints and nudges him.* GAVIN *takes one and drinks it, the others watching.*

In the event of anybody breaking the pattern, the others do all they can to make him conform.

We see GAVIN *placing the glass, empty now, on the counter. The other glasses are empty, too, and we see that he has caught up with them. His face is showing signs of the strain, though the others are in control of all their faculties, even if they are noisy and talkative, as we resume natural sound.*

1 TERRY. He's a pudding.

2 DAVE. Big onion.

3 KEN. Got a good left foot.

4 TERRY. It's only to stop him falling over.

5 FRANK. Only got one this season and that went off his bum ...

6 TERRY. Never see him grafting midfield ...

7 KEN. He's a striker.

8 DAVE. Plays like he's on strike.

9 FRANK. I wouldn't pay him in washers.

10 TERRY. Wouldn't pay any of 'em, they're all rubbish.

11 GAVIN. Excuse me.

12 TERRY. Why? What did you do?

13 DAVE. I can't smell anything.

14 GAVIN. Are we talking about football?

His speech is slurred enough for them to notice and send him up.

15 TERRY. Yesh.

16 KEN. Thatsh what we're chalking about, yes ...

17 DAVE. Rovers, biggest load of rubbish in Third Division ...

18 FRANK. They're all cripples, not their fault ...

19 TERRY. Pathetic, they are ...

20 DAVE. Play like a load of women.

21 GAVIN. I see. I wonder whether we might go. I'd be very interested to see ...

22 TERRY. To put in your book?

23 GAVIN. Possibly.

24 TERRY. Put Rovers in your book, you'll get it banned.

25 GAVIN. Obviously you're not very interested, if they're as bad as you say ... but if you could direct me.

26 DAVE. Course we're going, we always go ...

> GAVIN *doesn't begin to understand why they should always go to see a lousy team.*

1   GAVIN. I see. [*He doesn't.*] Good.

2   TERRY. We generally pop in Danny's shop on the way down.

3   GAVIN. I see. [*Again he doesn't, but he is gaining confidence.*] What does Danny sell in his shop?

> *The question provokes a burst of laughter.*

4   KEN. He doesn't sell nowt . . . he gives money away.

> *An even bigger burst of laughter and we see the group of faces from* GAVIN's *viewpoint; laughing at his ignorance, laughing with his innocence—sympathetic and aggressive.*

THE BETTING SHOP   Day

> *Opening with a close shot on* GAVIN, *as if reacting to the lads' faces, then he screws up his eyes, trying to focus on something at a greater distance. We see the object of his attention: the large blackboard in the betting shop on a busy Saturday afternoon when there are six meetings on. The board is a mass of information: results, odds, runners, S.P.'s, etc. Against this, we hear the running commentary on the tannoy, a permanent theme beneath the dialogue—and* GAVIN *doesn't understand any of it.*
> *The dialogue is more like a series of monologues: nobody is really talking to anybody else, with obvious exceptions. The shop is small, smokey and crowded.*

5   DAVE. Two pound overweight Kestrel.

6   TERRY. Can't do the distance.

7   KEN. Acts on any going.

8   FRANK [*to* GAVIN]. Do you believe in magic?

9   GAVIN [*smiling*]. I'm beginning to.

10   DAVE. Mind you, Lester's the lad.

11   FRANK. Give us a quid then.

> GAVIN *gives* FRANK *a pound.* FRANK *goes to the counter.*

12   TERRY. You're a mug, professor.

1   GAVIN. Eh?

   But TERRY *is absorbed in his own problems again.*

2   TERRY. Beaten a length last time out.

3   KEN. He's bent, is that trainer.

4   DAVE. Shortening, look. Down to twos.

5   TERRY. Get in quick.

6   DAVE. Taking a price me.

7   KEN. Settle for S.P.

   DAVE *moves away from the group, to the counter.*

8   TERRY. Wouldn't touch it with a bargepole.

9   KEN. Six to four now.

10 TERRY. False favourite.

11 KEN. Hasn't come all the way from Newmarket just for its oats.

   KEN *moves away from the group as* DAVE *rejoins it.*

12 DAVE. I'm a mug, what am I?

13 TERRY. It's the going, kid, too soft.

14 DAVE. I fancy Lewis's in the next.

15 TERRY. Donkey.

16 DAVE. Mile and half's a bit too far.

17 TERRY. Saw it racing on Scarborough sands last year.

18 GAVIN [*looking round, a little anxious*]. I gave him a pound.

   KEN *rejoins the group as* TERRY *moves away.*

19 KEN. Eh?

20 GAVIN. Magic he said. I gave him a pound.

21 KEN. Magic, right. The disappearing quid. I said Lester.

22 DAVE. *I* said Lester.

23 KEN. I didn't do it.

24 DAVE. Me neither.

1   KEN. Want your brains washing. [*He indicates* GAVIN, *as if he were an object.*] He gives Frank a quid.

2   DAVE. Mug.

> FRANK *rejoins the group. He pushes two pound notes into* GAVIN's *top pocket.*

3   GAVIN. There's two. [*He counts them in awe and wonder.*] That's magic.

4   FRANK. I told you.

5   GAVIN. Do you say abracadabra?

6   FRANK. Say Lester.

7   GAVIN. What?

> GAVIN *is drunk, bewildered and happy. He beams at the world.*

THE FOOTBALL GROUND   Day.

> *First we see a general establishing shot of the local ground on match day—not Old Trafford or Goodison but a Third Division outfit like Halifax Town or Doncaster Rovers—with about 4000 people speckling the terraces. We do not need to see any of the play, maybe we simply see the teams running out and kicking in. Then we discover* DAVE, KEN, TERRY, FRANK *and* GAVIN *in a group on the end terracing. There is no natural sound though the four lads are shouting loudly and vigorously.* GAVIN *does not shout. He leans on the barrier, feeling not too well and slowly subsiding beneath a combination of alienation and wanting to be sick. Against this sequence we hear* GAVIN's *voice over.*

8   GAVIN. Professional sport plays a central part in the working-class Saturday, whether in the form of organized gambling on horse-racing or watching the local football team. It is obvious that the latter sport is in difficulties and public interest is declining. While successful teams in the First Division are prospering, teams in the lower divisions no longer command unquestioning loyalty except for a hard core of enthusiasts.

> GAVIN *taps* DAVE *on the shoulder.* DAVE *nods towards one side of the*

terracing, and we watch GAVIN's *unsteady but urgent journey along the terrace, up and over the top.*
Cut to a medium shot of a corrugated iron structure with the word Gents painted on in big, bold lettering that wouldn't win any Design Centre award, then slowly pan across to discover GAVIN *sitting on the rough flight of steps at the rear of the terracing. We go closer to him as he leans forward, head in hands, waiting for the world to slow down a bit so he can resume normal living.*

1 GAVIN. [*voice over*]. But among this hardcore of supporters, there is total identification with the local team. Every kick is scrutinized with passion. Above all, everybody has a good time. This is the place to enjoy yourself.

THE LIVING-ROOM   Day

DAVE *and* GAVIN *sit in the respective armchairs,* DAVE's *attention on the television set which is showing the fag end of the afternoon's sports coverage.* GAVIN *still looks pale and wan.*

2 DAVE. Look at that . . . hardly a single favourite gone in . . .

MRS MILNER *comes through from the kitchen and, inevitably, starts to set the table.*

3 MRS MILNER. Bacon and eggs all right for tea, you lads?

4 DAVE. Aye, smashing, thanks Mam.

5 MRS MILNER. Gavin?

6 DAVE. And a few chips, eh?

7 MRS MILNER. All right for you, love?

8 GAVIN [*uneasily*]. I think, if it's all right by you, I'll go and lie down for a little while . . .

9 MRS MILNER. Do you feel all right?

10 GAVIN. I'm all right, just I feel a little . . .

11 DAVE. Feels a bit lousy . . . off you go, kid, you've got till six o'clock . . .

GAVIN *gets up and goes out.*

12 MRS MILNER. What have you been doing to him?

1 DAVE. Couple of drinks and a football match, what's wrong with that? We still get egg and chips, even if Einstein's feeling poorly, do we?

2 MRS MILNER. Hardly worth it, your dad not here and . . .

3 DAVE. Hey. [*He pulls a wad of notes from his back pocket, peels off a fiver and gives it to his mother.*] Present.

4 MRS MILNER. From you?

5 DAVE. From Geoff Lewis.

MRS MILNER *crosses to the kitchen.*

And make it two eggs, eh? I'll have his.

DAVE *settles down in his chair with the evening paper and a look of great self-satisfaction. We hear* GAVIN's *voice over.*

6 GAVIN. Among certain sectors of the working-class population there is an apparently limitless capacity for eating and drinking.

THE BEDROOM   Day

GAVIN *lies on the bed, speaking into the tape-recorder.*

7 GAVIN. Indeed, my own personal experience to date suggests they never stop . . . if they're not bloody well eating, they're bloody well drinking . . . [*The thought is a little too much. He switches off the tape-recorder but he carries on talking to himself.*] Chops and mashed potato and five more pints please, Ted, and eggs and bacon and five more pints, please, Ted, and how about some chips and five more pints please, Ted . . .

There is a knock at the door.

Come in.

DAVE *comes in with a cup of tea.*

8 DAVE. Mam says here's a cup of tea.

9 GAVIN [*sits up*]. Thanks.

10 DAVE. Wasn't sure whether you took sugar so we put a couple in.

Hint of agony on GAVIN's *face but it goes unnoticed.*

1 GAVIN [*takes the tea*]. Thanks.

2 DAVE. You see the pale patches? [*He refers to the pale patches on the wall.*]

3 GAVIN. Yes.

4 DAVE. Pin-ups . . . like birds with nothing on. Mam took them down, she thought they might upset you.

5 GAVIN. Not a chance.

6 DAVE. They're in that top drawer if you're interested. [*He indicates a drawer in the wardrobe.*] Ready in half an hour?

7 GAVIN. Ready for what?

8 DAVE. Saturday night? . . .

9 GAVIN. Oh . . . the usual . . .

10 DAVE [*laughs*]. Cheer up, it might never happen.

11 GAVIN. If it doesn't happen, there's no point in going out.

12 DAVE. You dirty dog. See you, kid.

DAVE *goes out.* GAVIN *sips the tea but doesn't like it much.*

THE CLUB Night
GAVIN *sits at a table in the Club Bar with* TERRY, KEN, FRANK *and* DAVE—*who at this moment is placing the inevitable tray of pints on the table at the completion of his journey from the bar. We hear* GAVIN's *voice over.*

13 GAVIN. Saturday night is very much like Saturday mid-day, except that it is dark outside.

The lads pick up their pints.

14 TERRY. Cheers, Dave . . .

15 KEN and FRANK. Cheers kid.

16 GAVIN. Cheers.

17 DAVE. Up yours.

18 TERRY. Have you finished your book yet?

19 GAVIN. Not quite.

1 TERRY. Dragging on a bit, isn't it?

2 KEN. Is Rovers going to be in it?

3 FRANK. When big Smithy stuck one on that centre half?

4 DAVE. He was a mucky beggar, that, wasn't he?

5 TERRY. Ref was blind an' all . . .

6 KEN. Full back should have been off for a start.

7 FRANK. Right over the top, every time, wasn't he?

8 TERRY. Smithy sorted him out an' all, didn't he?

9 KEN. I could hear the crunch where I was stood.

10 TERRY [*to* GAVIN]. Getting all this down are you?

11 GAVIN. It's very interesting.

12 KEN. Where do you come from?

13 GAVIN. Oxford.

14 DAVE. He's my friend from Oxford, I told you . . .

15 GAVIN. My parents live at East Grinstead.

16 FRANK. Have they got a team?

17 TERRY. You've heard of East Grinstead Dynamos, haven't
you?

18 KEN. What's that?

19 TERRY. Hockey team.

20 DAVE. Mixed.

21 TERRY. You what?

22 DAVE. Mixed hockey . . .

23 TERRY. Fellers and birds . . .?

24 DAVE. Why not?

25 FRANK. Sounds great.

26 KEN. Wouldn't mind being an overlapping defender . . . hey
up . . .

They laugh. KEN *goes to the bar.*

27 TERRY. I've never heard of East Grinstead.

28 GAVIN. It's rather dull. I prefer Oxford.

1   FRANK. Tried to back Oxford in the Boat Race last year . . .
Danny wouldn't have it . . .

2   DAVE. Why not?

3   FRANK. No each way bets he said.

4   DAVE. Bloody onion.

5   TERRY. Any road, you tell me what you want to know and
I'll see you're properly informed, kid . . .

6   GAVIN. Thank you.

7   DAVE. Rubbish.

8   FRANK, Aye, take no notice of Terry, he's stupid.

9   DAVE. He can only read in the dark.

     Pause. GAVIN *buys it.*

10 GAVIN. Is that right?

11 TERRY. Yes. I went to night school.

     KEN *returns with another tray of pints. As earlier,* GAVIN *is slipping
behind.*

12 DAVE ⎫
     TERRY ⎬ [*together*]. Cheers, kid.
     FRANK ⎭

13 KEN. Cheers.

14 GAVIN. I'll catch up.

15 DAVE. Best take your time.

16 TERRY. Come on then, ask me some questions.

17 GAVIN. Right. Question number one. What is . . . 'the usual'?

18 TERRY. You what?

19 GAVIN. What is it? What happens tonight?

20 TERRY. Oh I see . . .

21 DAVE. We have a few bevvies, like, then we go upstairs.

22 GAVIN. Upstairs?

23 DAVE. Yes.

24 GAVIN. What happens upstairs?

1   DAVE. There's a dance upstairs.

2   TERRY. You know what happens at dances . . .

3   GAVIN. People dance.

4   KEN. You look for something, don't you?

Pause.

5   GAVIN. Crumpet?

6   TERRY. Do they have it in East Grinstead?

7   GAVIN. I expect so, under a different name.

8   DAVE. There you are then, kid, now you know.

9   FRANK. Gerrit down in the book.

10   GAVIN. What time does it start, the dancing? . . .

11   DAVE [*looks at his watch*]. Hell's teeth . . .

12   TERRY. What's up? [*He looks at the time.*]

13   DAVE. Come on.

14   KEN. Started already.

They all drink up, except GAVIN.

15   FRANK. If you're not early, you miss it . . .

16   KEN. You don't get fixed up.

17   DAVE. Nowt left on the stall, you know . . .

18   TERRY. Coming?

They all get up, GAVIN *indicates the two pints, still untouched.*

19   GAVIN. I'll come up in a minute.

20   DAVE. Don't be too long, it won't come looking for you . . .

They all leave. GAVIN *sits. He picks up the first of the pints, takes a modest drink. His eyes look around the room, unlike lunchtime, there are women present, and he does a doubletake as he recognizes some-body coming in. It is* BETTY, *who walks across to the table.*

21   BETTY. On your own?

22   GAVIN [*stands up*]. Yes.

23   BETTY. Sit down.

1   GAVIN. I was going to bow.

2   BETTY. Don't be daft.

    They both sit down—not too close, not too intimate.

    With Dave, are you?

3   GAVIN. They've all gone upstairs.

4   BETTY. They're all mad.

5   GAVIN. I'm joining them . . . when I've caught up . . . [*indicating the pints*] . . . would you like one?

6   BETTY. I don't drink beer. [*This is half a hint.*]

7   GAVIN. Would you like a drink?

8   BETTY. Thought you'd never ask. Gin and orange please. Is that O.K?

9   GAVIN. On Lester.

    GAVIN *takes the two pound notes out of his top pocket to demonstrate his wealth. Then he crosses to the bar. We watch him as he waits to be served. In the background we see* BETTY *sitting at the table. The sound fades to a subdued murmur as we hear* GAVIN's *voice over.*

    In any society it is important to decide whether the male or the female is the dominant sex.

    We go closer to BETTY, *watching him, and we're pretty damn sure of the answer.*

    Fade out.

Fade in.

    Some time later GAVIN *is carrying a couple of shorts across to the table where* BETTY *is sitting. The number of empty glasses on the table tells us they've been there some time, though neither of them is drunk—only talkative.*

10   BETTY. Thanks, love. Cheers.

11   GAVIN. Cheers.

    A pause and a brief, shared smile.

12   BETTY. First time I've ever been boozing with anybody clever.

1 GAVIN. What about Sid?

2 BETTY. What do you know about Sid?

3 GAVIN. I know he exists.

4 BETTY. That'll do. All you need to know.

Pause.

5 GAVIN. Would you like to go upstairs to the dance?

6 BETTY. What for?

7 GAVIN. Well . . . to dance . . .

8 BETTY. No. [*She laughs at his unease.*] Not like Oxford is it?

9 GAVIN. Or East Grinstead.

10 BETTY. If it was Oxford and I was some pretty young student, what would you be saying to me?

11 GAVIN. I'd say . . . how about coming round to my place . . .?

12 BETTY. Oh aye. [*Pause.*] But you haven't got a place.

13 GAVIN. Not here. No. [*He smiles, a little warily.*] Problem, that.

14 BETTY [*matter-of-fact*]. I've got a place.

We hold GAVIN's *reaction, mingled delight and apprehension. Then, as we hear* GAVIN's *voice over, we watch them leave the club.*

15 GAVIN. There is some confusion over what, in terms of Saturday night, constitutes what is known as 'the usual'. To paraphrase Doctor Johnson, it is not perhaps Saturday night as it is . . .

As they go out, TERRY *sees them and we briefly hold his reaction.*

BETTY'S LIVING-ROOM Night

GAVIN's *voice continues over as we briefly explore the room before ending on a close shot of* GAVIN *as he watches* BETTY *tidying away odd newspapers to make the place look presentable.*

16 GAVIN. . . . but Saturday night as they would like it to be. As we would like it to be.

17 BETTY [*sits down*]. Kettle's on, won't take a minute.

Now we get a longer look at the room. Essentially it is the same as MRS MILNER's *in size and shape, but less crammed—no dining table—and the furniture is a couple of decades later in mass-produced concept.*

1 GAVIN. It's very similar to your mother's house, isn't it?

2 BETTY. Houses round here, they're all alike . . . rotten.

3 GAVIN. I wouldn't say that, it's very . . .

4 BETTY. Don't say homely or I'll belt your head in. [*Pause.*] How do you come to be staying with me mam?

5 GAVIN. Well I wanted to write this thesis about the infra-structure of . . .

6 BETTY. The what?

7 GAVIN. Infrastructure.

8 BETTY. We had one but it died. How do you come to be staying with me mam I said?

9 GAVIN. Your mother does cleaning for some people called Matthews . . .

10 BETTY. I've heard of them. Up near the golf course.

11 GAVIN. My father and Mr Matthews have got some sort of business tie-up . . . it was arranged through them . . .

12 BETTY. *What* was arranged?

13 GAVIN. Well . . . my coming here . . . so I could spend a bit of time living in a working-class community in 1972 . . . few days now just to do some preliminary research . . . then a longer period later . . .

14 BETTY. All about this infra . . . what?

15 GAVIN. Infrastructure.

16 BETTY. You're funny, aren't you? [*She laughs.*]

17 GAVIN. I don't think so.

18 BETTY. Us sweating blood to get out of here and you . . . funny, is that.

19 GAVIN. I'm on *your* side.

20 BETTY [*flatly*]. Ta.

1 GAVIN. Is that the kettle?

> *As there is a whistling from the kitchen.* BETTY *goes through and she continues the conversation through the open door as she makes a pot of tea.*

2 BETTY. I'll tell you what else makes me laugh.

3 GAVIN. What?

4 BETTY. You can fix it, through your dad, for you to stay at my mam's house . . .

5 GAVIN. Yes.

6 BETTY. But I couldn't fix it through my dad for me to stay in your mam's house. . .

> BETTY *comes into the living-room with tea and cups on a tray which she sets down in front of the fire on the floor.*

7 GAVIN. You're not laughing.

8 BETTY. You what?

9 GAVIN. You said it made you laugh.

10 BETTY. It doesn't really. [*Pause.*] You take things too seriously, love.

11 GAVIN. Sorry. Is that Sid on the mantelpiece?

12 BETTY. Yes.

13 GAVIN. Where is he?

14 BETTY. Working away. Scotland.

15 GAVIN. What's he do?

16 BETTY. Steel erector.

17 GAVIN. Isn't there any steel to erect nearer home?

18 BETTY. Work away you can get twice the money. There's no money in this town.

19 GAVIN. How often does he get home?

20 BETTY. Now and again. [*She is deliberately vague and unhelpful. She pours the tea.*]

21 GAVIN. What if he walked in now?

> *And it is a charming and innocent domestic scene.*

1 BETTY. He'd half kill you. Then he'd half kill me. Sugar?

2 GAVIN. No thank you.

INSIDE THE CLUB   Night

DAVE *joins* TERRY *and* KEN *at the bar.*

3 DAVE [*to barman*]. Twenty woods please . . . [*to the lads*] How you doing?

4 TERRY. Terrible.

5 KEN. Mine said she would have but she's got a slipped disc, so I said forget it . . .

6 DAVE. Where's Frank?

7 TERRY. He got fixed up early doors . . .

8 DAVE. He would. Ta [*as the cigs arrive*].

9 KEN. You haven't asked about your friend from Oxford.

10 DAVE. Einstein? Where's he gone?

11 KEN. Went off with your Betty.

12 DAVE [*surprised and impressed*]. Did he? Cheeky sod.

13 TERRY. Good job Sid's away.

14 DAVE. Stands to reason. She wouldn't have done it if Sid was at home. Daft talk, is that.

15 TERRY. Talking daft's what I'm best at.

16 KEN. That's true.

17 DAVE. I thought he'd got my room for the night but me mam says he's stopping the week.

18 TERRY. You what?

19 DAVE. Oh nowt. Hey up, there's a passionate bird waiting for me out there. . .

DAVE *dashes off.* TERRY *and* KEN *silently contemplate their pints.*

20 TERRY. Well kid?

21 KEN. What?

22 TERRY. Fish and chips and home is it?

205

Pause. KEN *contemplates the alternatives but there are none.*

1 KEN. I reckon.

They drink up.

THE LIVING-ROOM Night

GAVIN *and* BETTY *sit side by side on the settee in front of the fire. There is no physical contact but there is the emotional intimacy of people talking, heart to heart, in the small hours.*

2 BETTY. It'll be all over the street tomorrow . . . me coming in the club on my own . . .

3 GAVIN. Is it not done?

4 BETTY. Some of the women do it . . . if their husbands are away, working, or at sea, something like that . . . one or two of them have got fellers inside, well . . . can't blame them. But people do . . .

5 GAVIN. What? Blame them?

6 BETTY. Yes. See what they want to see. [*Pause.*] Go in with your family, that's all right. I thought mam and dad might be in.

7 GAVIN. But they weren't.

8 BETTY. No. Just my friend from Oxford.

9 GAVIN. See what they want to see.

10 BETTY. Eh?

11 GAVIN. Will *that* be all over the street.

12 BETTY. Me and you pushing off?

13 GAVIN. What'll they say about that?

14 BETTY. Depends what they think of you doesn't it?

15 GAVIN. I suppose so. [*He hesitates.*] I wonder what they think of me. . .

16 BETTY. Not much.

GAVIN *is taken aback by this abrupt assessment.*

17 GAVIN. Really?

1   BETTY. Well, you talk posh and you dress a bit pansified . . . they'll reckon you're a bit of a poof I daresay.

2   GAVIN. I'm not.

3   BETTY. Not saying you are. And no need to prove it . . . just . . . you asked me and I told you.

4   GAVIN. But your reputation's safe . . .

5   BETTY. As much as anybody's is.

6   GAVIN. I mean, I don't want to spell it out but . . . [*Again he hesitates.*]

7   BETTY. But what?

8   GAVIN. You invited me.

9   BETTY. Just thought . . . be nice to have a cup of tea not . . . not on my own.

10   GAVIN. That's fair. [*Pause.*] Is it worth it?

11   BETTY. What?

12   GAVIN. Worth the extra money your husband makes . . . being on your own?

13   BETTY. You don't make the rules, do you?

14   GAVIN. Rules?

15   BETTY. Live in a house like this, the rules say get a better house . . . can't do that without money . . . got to have the deposit and that . . . it's all money, everything's money.

16   GAVIN. It doesn't have to be.

17   BETTY. Can you manage without it?

18   GAVIN. Well, no, but. . .

19   BETTY. So we've all got to get as much as we can, haven't we?

20   GAVIN. Stand on your own feet?

21   BETTY. And on other people's, they reckon. Your dad must have done all right, didn't he?

22   GAVIN. Yes. He does all right.

No reactions from BETTY.

Don't you want to know what he does?

1   BETTY. Not particularly.

2   GAVIN. You're all a bit like that aren't you?

3   BETTY. Like what?

4   GAVIN. Selectively curious.

5   BETTY. I'm not as clever as you . . .

6   GAVIN. Only interested in certain things . . . like your brother's
     friends . . . they talk all the time, very knowledgeably,
     about football and racing and . . .

7   BETTY. And sex. . .

8   GAVIN. But that's about all. I mean, they're not very inter-
     ested in what I'm doing . . . it's . . . oh, writing a book are
     you, great . . . and then on with the football again or
     the birds . . .

9   BETTY. Well what it is, love . . . we're very interested in the
     things we're interested in . . . and not very interested in
     the things we're not interested in. [*She is quite proud of this.*]
     That's clever, that, isn't it?

10   GAVIN [*smiles*]. Beautifully put.

11   BETTY. I've put something beautifully.

     A shared smile.

12   GAVIN [*changing tack suddenly, almost professionally*].   If it's money
     you need, couldn't you get a job?

13   BETTY. I do, off and on.

14   GAVIN.   What sort of work?

15   BETTY. Stand there gawping at a machine. If it breaks down,
     you fetch a feller, he fixes it. Then you watch it again.
     Went on short time two months ago, then I got the
     sack . . . not having been there long . . . last in, first out.
     Another cup of tea?

16   GAVIN. No thanks.

17   BETTY. Plenty in the pot.

18   GAVIN. I'm all right thanks.

19   BETTY. Pity to waste it . . . [*She pours herself another cup.*]

1   GAVIN. Would you say you were lonely?

2   BETTY. Sometimes, I suppose. Course, it's different for a woman isn't it?

3   GAVIN. How is it?

4   BETTY. I can't go in a pub on my own without them thinking I'm on the game or something . . . and I don't want to join the darts team . . . but fellers can go anywhere . . . and if they're after a bit of you know . . . well everybody laughs, it's clever if it's a bloke . . . [*Pause*.] But it's just somebody to talk to. To talk rubbish to. Doesn't have to be *about* anything. I'd say to Sid sometimes . . . how about talking? And he'd say what about? And I'd say not *about* anything . . . just talk . . . you know what I mean?

5   GAVIN. I think so.

6   BETTY. Not just Sid . . . *all* fellers . . . they won't talk unless it's *about* something . . . clever fellers especially . . .

7   GAVIN. And you just want to talk?

8   BETTY. Doesn't matter what about. I can't tell you a thing I've said since we got in . . . daft, isn't it?

9   GAVIN. Not in the least.

10 BETTY. You're not fed up?

11 GAVIN. No.

12 BETTY. You're a good listener.

13 GAVIN. That's why I'm here.

   Pause.

14 BETTY. Bit lonely yourself, aren't you?

15 GAVIN [*cautious*]. I wouldn't say so. . .

16 BETTY. Only child?

17 GAVIN. Yes.

   BETTY *laughs*.

   How do you know?

1   BETTY. Don't know. Anything you wanted you could
    have . . . ?

2   GAVIN. When I was a child.

3   BETTY. Then it changes.

4   GAVIN. Then it changes. [*Pause. Another shared moment as he echoes
    her words.*] I would like . . . [*He hesitates.*]

5   BETTY. What?

    GAVIN *moves nearer to her and puts his arm round her.*

6   GAVIN. To do that.

7   BETTY. Just that . . .

8   GAVIN. Just that.

9   BETTY. What's wrong with a cuddle?

10 GAVIN [*relaxing*]. Exactly.

    They lean back on the settee. She rests her head on his shoulder.

    That's the trouble with an electric fire.

11 BETTY. What is?

12 GAVIN. You can't see pictures in it.

13 BETTY. You can get them with like artificial coal.

14 GAVIN. Artificial pictures.

    Pause.

15 BETTY. I don't go to the pictures much.

    They laugh, quietly and together.

16 GAVIN. Don't mean that sort of pictures. [*He slips into a send-up
    Yorkshire accent.*] You're a bit daft, aren't you?

17 BETTY. You've got to be daft to live round here.

18 GAVIN. That's what the pictures are about.

19 BETTY. What?

20 GAVIN. Oh . . . some sort of world where I don't have a better
    house than you . . . and where you don't have to sweat
    and slave getting the money you need to buy a better
    house.

1   BETTY. We don't slave . . . we're not that stupid . . . you get
    away with what you can . . .

2   GAVIN. But it could all be better, couldn't it?

3   BETTY. Who's going to change it?

4   GAVIN [*awkwardly*]. Well . . .

5   BETTY. You?

    GAVIN *shrugs*

    And whose army?

6   GAVIN. It's what I believe.

7   BETTY. You're talking *about* things again . . .

8   GAVIN. Instead of just talking?

9   BETTY. Instead of just talking.

10 GAVIN. I'm sorry. [*He hesitates then takes the plunge.*] Give us a kiss,
    luv.

    And they kiss, long and slow and gentle. We hear GAVIN'*s voice over.*

11 GAVIN. The surprising thing is that among the closely knit
    family circles there are individual examples of intense
    personal loneliness.

    They break off. She looks at him, hard.

12 BETTY. Will you put this in your book?

13 GAVIN. What?

14 BETTY. This. Is this part of the infra thing . . . ?

15 GAVIN. Infrastructure . . . I . . . er, don't know. . .

    She breaks away from him abruptly.

16 BETTY. That's it, then, isn't it?

17 GAVIN. I'm sorry I . . .

18 BETTY. The right answer was no.

19 GAVIN. That's what I meant.

20 BETTY. Not now, when you've had time to think about it.
    [*Pause.*] The answer was no.

A long silence.

1   GAVIN. So I might as well go home.

2   BETTY. You're a long way from home.

3   GAVIN. Your mother's house.

4   BETTY. You can grow wings and fly to the moon as far as I'm concerned.

GAVIN gets up and crosses to the door.

5   GAVIN. It shouldn't be like this.

6   BETTY. Wasn't us made it like this. You and your old man made it like this.

GAVIN nods, acknowledging the point.

7   GAVIN. It's daft.

He goes out. BETTY stays beside the mantelpiece.

8   BETTY [*to herself*]. It's daft all right.

We hold her in close-up as she slowly and unemotionally clears away the tea things. We hear GAVIN's voice over.

9   GAVIN. At night, the open-hearted warmth and friendliness seem to disappear. The streets are dark and menacing.

THE LIVING-ROOM   Night

Now we are looking at MILNER, in his working clothes, sitting in his armchair—a long look at a worker's face as we hear GAVIN's voice continuing over.

10 GAVIN. It is almost as if the streets, and its inhabitants, are preparing their defences for a battle.

MILNER looks up as GAVIN comes in.

11 MILNER. Hello, lad.

12 GAVIN. Hello, Mr Milner. Didn't think you'd be up...

13 MILNER. Oh aye. Just got in from work.

14 GAVIN [*puzzled*]. Work?

15 MILNER. Two till ten but I did extra half-shift...

1 GAVIN. I see. [*He doesn't quite.*] I read an article not long ago about the disruptive effects of the shift system on family life.

2 MILNER. It helps productivity. Efficient use of mechanical plant. The management gives us little books explaining it all. [*Pause.*] We make them pay, like . . .

3 GAVIN. Quite right too.

4 MILNER. Oh aye, of course, you're on our side, aren't you?

5 GAVIN. Yes.

6 MILNER [*smiles*]. Have you had a good day?

7 GAVIN. Exhausting.

8 MILNER. What's exhausted you?

9 GAVIN. I seem to have drunk a lot of beer for one thing . . .

10 MILNER. Our Dave hasn't come in yet, he must be doing all right.

GAVIN *is trying to sort out his memories of the day.*

11 GAVIN. We went to the football match.

12 MILNER. Good match?

13 GAVIN. Didn't see all that much of it . . .

14 MILNER. You're lucky, from what I hear.

15 GAVIN. Oh yes, and I backed a horse . . .

16 MILNER. Good lad . . . did you get a good price?

17 GAVIN. Good price? Well no, what happened was . . . one of Dave's friends took a pound off me and came back a few minutes later and gave me two pounds back . . . and said thank Lester. I didn't fully understand what was going on really.

MILNER *smiles and picks up the local Saturday night sports paper—the 'green 'un'—and checks the racing results.*

18 MILNER. One of Dave's mates?

19 GAVIN. Frank I think they called him.

20 MILNER. He owes you thirty-six bob.

1   GAVIN. One pound eighty.

2   MILNER. Thirty-six bob, I don't recognize the metric system just like I don't recognize time and motion and people measuring how fast I work, all ends up with one of us getting the elbow. I say thirty-six bob.

3   GAVIN. How come he owes me thirty-six bob?

4   MILNER. Only had one winner, did Lester . . . two fifteen. . .

5   GAVIN. Yes, it would be about quarter past two. . .

6   MILNER. Won at three to one . . . so that's three quid to come plus your stake, less your tax . . . three pounds sixteen you should have had. . . .

7   GAVIN. Two pounds he gave me.

8   MILNER. Done you, hasn't he?

9   GAVIN. Must have made a mistake.

10   MILNER. No he didn't. He kept it.

11   GAVIN. I see. [*He's hurt by the thought.*] Well, if he needs the money . . .

12   MILNER. He doesn't need the money.

13   GAVIN. So why did he keep it?

14   MILNER. Oh I daresay he was striking a blow for working-class solidarity against the bourgeoisie. . .

Pause. GAVIN *is startled by* MILNER's *sudden lurch into political language.*

15   GAVIN. I didn't know you were a political man, Mr Milner. . .

16   MILNER. No, I'm not. I mean, if the union say out, I'll be out . . . but that's as far as it goes . . . in the war I took an interest. In the army, out in the desert . . . lot of time to waste between battles, you know? We'd have talks and discussions about it all . . . what the war was about . . . what sort of world we'd make . . . [*Pause.*] We got very near it, you know that? Very near it. But there's all the city gents in their big boots waiting to kick it all to bits the minute they get the chance. Your people.

17   GAVIN. Not my people.

1   MILNER. No? Well, too late for arguments now. . .

2   GAVIN. Don't you talk about it usually?

3   MILNER. Not here, no. Mam says shuttup and Dave, he thinks politicians are all out to line their pockets and happen he's right. Get yourself in the Cabinet, write your memoirs and retire, it's not bad, is it? [*Pause.*] And you get tired. Too many night shifts.

4   GAVIN. So *you've* retired?

5   MILNER. I like to know the rules, even if I don't play. I don't back horses, but I understand the system.

6   GAVIN. Don't you want to change the system?

7   MILNER. Not if you think about it. There's your two per cent up there that's got all the money . . . and there's us down here . . . what happens? Are those gentlemen going to share it all out with all of us out of the kindness of their hearts? Well?

8   GAVIN. No. Obviously not.

9   MILNER. So are we going to take off them?

10 GAVIN. Why not?

11 MILNER. We don't shoot gentlemen in England, we raise our hats to them.

12 GAVIN. Even though you know all the time what's going on?

13 MILNER. Did you enjoy your dinner today?

14 GAVIN. I'm sorry I . . .

15 MILNER. Straight question . . . did you enjoy your dinner?

16 GAVIN. Yes. It was fine.

17 MILNER. Our mam doesn't usually cook dinner on a Saturday. We have fish and chips from round the corner.

18 GAVIN. I like fish and chips.

19 MILNER. She cooked dinner 'cause you were here. Smart, well-spoken, good manners . . . all that. A gent. She knows a gent when she sees one. Knows how to behave. Well, she does cleaning for your father's friends . . . Mr and Mrs Matthews . . .

1 GAVIN. Mr Matthews isn't exactly a friend, he's a . . .

2 MILNER. What? What is he?

3 GAVIN. Business associate.

4 MILNER. Aye aye.

5 GAVIN [*smiles*]. Am I wasting my time?

6 MILNER. What? Writing your book?

7 GAVIN. If you're saying that . . . well, the way you all behave
    when I'm here isn't the way you behave when I'm not
    here. . .

8 MILNER. We're all a bit disruptive really. Tell us to smile at
    the camera we might make a face . . . our Dave had a
    job a bit back. Maintenance job on one of these old
    schools round here . . . primary school . . . hundred
    years old . . . you maybe haven't seen one of them. . .

9 GAVIN. My school was three hundred years old. . .

10 MILNER. Ah but when it's that old, it's like vintage, part of
    our island heritage . . . not this one Dave was in . . . him
    and his mate, checking all the windows, see they open
    properly, no leaks and that . . . and this teacher says: 'I
    hope you men aren't going to be disrupting my work
    for too long . . . ' High and mighty, you know?

11 GAVIN. I know.

12 MILNER. Well there was nowt wrong in her classroom so our
    Dave gets his knife and puts it through the sash cord on
    one of the windows . . . took them half a day to fix it . . .
    [*Pause.*] Funny lad is our Dave. Doesn't like anybody
    talking down to him.

13 GAVIN. I wouldn't even try.

14 MILNER. Am I spoiling your book?

15 GAVIN. No, you're helping it a lot.

16 MILNER. Good.

17 GAVIN. And you don't think it'll ever change?

18 MILNER. Maybe change round the edges a bit but . . . your
    people won't relinquish their power . . . our people

won't take it . . . your people'll go on saying we can have six per cent rises and we'll ask for fifteen and we'll settle for ten. . .

2 GAVIN. And your Dave'll put his knife through a few more sash cords?

3 MILNER. You won't stop him. Can't stop him. And your people'll keep your vintage schools open and teach you how to talk so our mam'll pretend we don't have fish and chips for dinner. . .

4 GAVIN. And the Daily Express will continue to say the class war is over.

5 MILNER. Well, I've got my telly. Got my football match and my pint of bitter . . . best bitter . . . the opium of the masses. That's not bad is it?

6 GAVIN. Not bad at all.

Pause.

7 MILNER. We know the terms. We know the rules. But we've never fought the war.

8 GAVIN. Why?

9 MILNER. Scared of losing. Or scared of winning. Not sure which. [*He looks at his watch.*] Getting early, time I was in bed.

MILNER *gets up and we watch him as he winds the clock on the mantelpiece and marginally corrects it. We stay close on* MILNER *as we hear* GAVIN's *voice over.*

10 GAVIN. Much of my research highlighted the problem of any researcher: is the subject speaking the truth?

THE BEDROOM   Night

GAVIN *is in bed, trying to sleep, but restless and half-awake as his voice continues over.*

To what extent do people distort what they say, or even tell deliberate lies, when they lack complete faith in the person asking the questions? In other words, what's the flaming point of it all?

There is a sudden, urgent knocking on the bedroom door.

2   DAVE [*outside the door*]. Are you awake, kid?

3   GAVIN [*stirs and sits up*]. What?

4   DAVE. Can I come in?

5   GAVIN [*puzzled*]. Yes, come in.

> DAVE *comes in, bright and cheerful like the day had just begun.* GAVIN *looks at him, bewildered, as* DAVE *switches on the light then sits down on the end of the bed.*

6   DAVE. What time's the first train?

7   GAVIN. What first train?

8   DAVE. Yours. Back home to East Wotsit. . .

9   GAVIN. Grinstead.

10   DAVE. Grinstead. What a daft name.

11   GAVIN. But I'm in Oxford anyway.

12   DAVE. Well you want to be there sharpish . . .

13   GAVIN. I don't know what you're talking about. . .

14   DAVE. I'm talking about Sid coming home, that's what I'm talking about. . .

15   GAVIN. Sid?

16   DAVE. Betty's feller. . .

17   GAVIN. What about it?

18   DAVE. You're not very bright considering you're brilliant . . . when he finds out you went home with her tonight. . .

19   GAVIN. All we did was . . . have a cup of tea.

> *Pause.* DAVE *looks at him.*

20   DAVE. All we did was have a cup of tea, Sid . . . Sid . . . put that axe down, Sid. . .

21   GAVIN. You're joking. . .

22   DAVE. You don't know him. . . He put a feller in hospital once. . .

1   GAVIN. Half killed him. . .

2   DAVE. That's right.

Pause.

3   GAVIN. What time's he coming home?

4   DAVE. Mid-morning. Got a lift on a lorry.

5   GAVIN. Trains are terrible on a Sunday.

6   DAVE. Sid's terrible on a Sunday an' all . . . especially if his missus's been having it off with . . .

7   GAVIN. Cup of tea I said . . .

8   DAVE. Not my fault if you're a mug. . . [*He gets up and crosses to the door.*] Any road . . . I've told you . . . don't blame me when he sticks the boot in.

9   GAVIN. All right. Message received and understood. [*He looks at his watch.*] By the way.

10   DAVE. What?

11   GAVIN. I think your mate owes me thirty-six bob.

12   DAVE [*laughs*]. Aye, that's right. He does. [*Pause.*] You try getting it. [*He goes out.*]

13   GAVIN [*voice over*]. There comes a point in any research project. . .

And as we hear his voice we watch him slowly get out of bed and start dressing.

. . . when one has to ask the question . . . is it worth it?

And there is a sudden burst of the noise of a train.

INSIDE A FIRST CLASS COMPARTMENT Day

We discover GAVIN *sitting in the corner seat. We do not see the first class sign at this point. He is alone, dictating into his tape-recorder.*

14   GAVIN. How far is one intruding into people's privacy? How far do they resist and distort what they say to the extent that what they say is worthless, in any realistic sociological context. [*He pauses for breath.*] It seems to me

possible ... probably ... that the study of working-class areas and lives will always fall down on this problem. Unless the researcher is totally accepted by the community, the community will tend to ... tend to stick a knife through his sash cords ... [*He smiles, pleased with the image.*] My final reflections on the study area are dominated by. . .

THE LIVING-ROOM   Day

The MILNERS' *living-room as* MRS MILNER *comes in carrying a bundle of fish and chips that she dumps on the table.*

2   GAVIN [*voice over*]. . . . the way in which the women of the area ultimately control the running of the home.

Then we see MILNER *come to the table, sitting down to his plate of fish and chips.*

The way the men, especially the older men, have a clear understanding of the world around them ... linked to a feeling that they will do nothing to fundamentally change it. . .

MR *and* MRS MILNER *exchange glances as they realize* DAVE *is not with them, though his fish and chips are.*

3   MRS MILNER. Where's our Dave?

THE CLUB   Day

We see a tray of pints moving round the inevitable circle: DAVE, TERRY, KEN *and* FRANK.

4   GAVIN [*voice over*]. The younger men are apparently friendly and generous but here, too, I felt that I wasn't always told the truth and the whole truth.

We pick up natural sound as the lads have a big laugh about something or other.

5   DAVE. So I told him Sid was coming home.
6   TERRY. Well he isn't, is he?

1 DAVE. Mebbe next week, or the week after. . .

2 KEN. Yer rotten sod.

3 DAVE. Well he'd got my room, hadn't he?

4 FRANK [*pansy voice*]. You'll never find a friend in Oxford now. . .

5 DAVE. Stuff Oxford. Stuff 'em all . . . [*Rapid change of subject but not out of embarrassment.*] Hey, what about this big nut they've signed from Sheffield United?

6 TERRY. Seen him. He's tripe.

7 KEN. Rubbish he is.

8 FRANK. What they paid? Ten thousand quid?

9 DAVE. Ten thousand washers more like. . .

THE LIVING-ROOM IN BETTY'S HOUSE   Day

10 GAVIN [*voice over*]. And there is the loneliness.

BETTY *sits in a chair at the fireside, drinking a cup of tea—not a soulful face, but blunt and matter-of-fact—just a girl having a cup of tea.*

Future plans. It is obvious that the most worthwhile research will be carried out where the researcher can most easily merge with the landscape.

BACK IN THE TRAIN   Day

11 GAVIN [*speaking into his tape recorder*]. Start new page. New heading. The Infrastructure of the Middle Class. Preliminary survey. [*Pause.*] East Grinstead.

He switches off the recorder. Packs away the mike. Sits back and relaxes. We move from his face to the 'First Class' sign on the window, which lurks behind the closing credits.

Fade out.

Topics for Discussion

and Written Work

EXCURSION

1   Norman says that a cup-tie is no place for a woman, and it is clear that the women on this excursion have little interest in football. Why do they go?

2   Would men be as willing to join a group of women for an outing of theirs? Discuss the difference in attitudes.

3   Although Terry's enthusiasm leads him to throw a few toilet rolls on to the pitch, the people on the train behave fairly well. Do you think that reports of vandalism by soccer enthusiasts are exaggerated?

4   Edie says that the men just live from one football match to the next. If our own jobs were more interesting would we still need recreation?

5   Now that television can provide better close-ups of the game, why do thousands of people still prefer to stand in the open for hours to see a match?

6   Tom says that the women live from one special offer to the next. Certainly Doris and Edie spend most of their time shopping. Do you think they could have spent their time in a strange town more usefully?

7   Write a short speech by the referee giving his thoughts when he was barracked by the crowd.

8   Tom and Arthur spend a lot of time remembering matches that took place years ago. Why?

ON CHRISTMAS DAY IN THE MORNING

9   Jones says that Christmas is 'just an orgy of self-indulgence'.
    Does he mean it? Do you agree with him?

10 More people are spending Christmas in hotels nowadays. Why?

11 When Wilson is interviewed by Morgan he suggests that

the thefts don't matter because the owners are insured. Do you agree?

12   Why should a man like Wilson who has had the benefit of a good education and background become a thief?

13   Yvonne, the maid, has a mother and baby to support. Does this justify her behaviour in helping the Wilsons to steal from people who are wealthy?

14   Write a short scene showing what happens when Watt interviews Yvonne, after the Wilsons have been arrested.

AND A LITTLE LOVE BESIDES

15   Carter appears to be cynical about the church. Why is he a vicar?

16   Is he the sort of vicar who would attract large congregations? Would you discuss personal problems with him?

17   Write a short description of the Friday Fellowship for the Parish Magazine
       (a) as seen by Amy
       (b) as seen by Hennessy.

18   Although this play has a serious theme, it is written in a light-hearted style. Describe any differences you would have made if you had.

19   The Hennessys and Mitchell don't show much charity towards Briggs. Why do you think they are members of the church?

SEVENTEEN PER CENT SAID PUSH OFF

20   Dave and his mates seem to spend most of their free time in pubs, dance halls, soccer grounds and betting shops. Do you think their behaviour is typical of young

people living in an industrial area? How else could they use their leisure time?

21   People often reveal details of their personal lives to television interviewers and newspaper reporters. Why do they do it? Would you find it easy to talk to somebody like Gavin?

22   One of the reasons for Betty's loneliness is that her husband is working away in Scotland. She says that she can't go into pubs on her own without people suspecting her motives: where could she meet people and make friends?

23   What are Gavin's reactions when Mr Milner tells him that Frank cheated him of part of his winnings? Would your reactions be the same?

24   Does our behaviour change when strangers are present? Write a short breakfast scene between Mr and Mrs Milner on their own and then the same scene with Gavin present.

25   Gavin has to remember that the Milner family call their mid-day meal dinner and not lunch. Can you think of other words or phrases which point to differences in social background?

Alan Plater was born in Jarrow in 1935, but his family moved to Hull when he was three. After leaving Kingston High School, Hull, he returned to the North East to study architecture at King's College, Newcastle-upon-Tyne, but did not qualify. He spent two years in an architect's office before deciding to work from home, drawing up plans for people who needed minor alterations to property, and was able to find time to combine his interest in architecture with writing.

His first play *The Smokeless Zone* was broadcast in 1961 and since then he has had several radio plays produced. His contact with the North Region of the B.B.C. naturally led him towards television and to a fruitful collaboration with Vivian Daniels, who directed most of his early work for the medium. Many authors are reluctant to write scripts for television series which are sometimes considered to rely so much on a format that the writer feels that he is working on a conveyor belt. Alan Plater, though, has always had a strong respect for *Z Cars*, for which he has written numerous scripts, and for its offspring *Softly Softly*, to which he still contributes. His interest has recently turned towards the cinema and since the success of his first film, an adaptation of D. H. Lawrence's *The Virgin and the Gipsy*, he has completed several original scripts.

Having opted out of the drift to London he has decided to stay in the North and much of his work for the stage has been written with particular regional theatres in mind: Peter Cheeseman directed several of his plays including *Ted's Cathedral* and *A Smashing Day* for the Victoria Theatre, Stoke-on-Trent; *Charlie Came to Our Town* was written for the Harrogate Festival; *Hop Step and Jump* and *See the Pretty Lights* were originally produced in the round at the Library Theatre, Scarborough, and *And a Little Love Besides* at the Arts Centre in Hull. Using some stories by Sid Chaplin about the mining community as a starting point, he wrote *Close the Coalhouse Door* for the Newcastle Playhouse. This documentary play, with songs by Alex Glasgow, packed the theatre for a long time and it has become an important milestone of the sixties. It is not surprising that when Bill Hays, who directed the show, was appointed Director of the new Leeds Playhouse, he commissioned the same team to write the opening production *Simon Says*.

Alan Plater was the original editor of the B.B.C.'s programme of new writing, *The Northern Drift*, which has given a first hearing to hundreds of young writers and was a driving force behind the creation of the Arts Centre in his home town, Hull.

He is a man with wide interests and spends much of his free time talking to people in schools, technical colleges, the local prison and to members of various societies. He has never been one of those writers who lives in an ivory tower remote from the real world; when he is not working you are most likely to find him at the greyhound stadium, attending a jazz concert, or pottering about at the caravan site where he spends free weekends with his young family.

OTHER RECOMMENDED PLAYS BY ALAN PLATER

A Quiet Night (in *Z Cars*, Longman)
The Mating Season (in *Worth a Hearing*, Blackie)
Close the Coalhouse Door (Methuen)
See the Pretty Lights (in *Theatre Choice*, Blackie)